The Tie That Binds

The Tie
That Binds

*Identity and Political Attitudes in the
Post–Civil Rights Generation*

Andrea Y. Simpson

NEW YORK UNIVERSITY PRESS

New York and London

NEW YORK UNIVERSITY PRESS
New York and London

Library of Congress Cataloging-in-Publication Data
Simpson, Andrea Y., 1954–
The tie that binds : identity and political attitudes in the post–
civil rights generation / Andrea Y. Simpson.
p.   cm.
Includes bibliographical references and index.
ISBN 0-8147-8101-2 (cloth : acid-free paper)
ISBN 0-8147-8102-0 (pbk. : acid-free paper)
1. Afro-Americans—Politics and government. 2. Conservatism—
United States. 3. Liberalism—United States. 4. United States—
Race relations—Political aspects. 5. United States—Politics
and government. I. Title. E185.615.S652   1998
305.896'073'09045—dc21   97-53762
                                        CIP

For Mr. Maloney

Contents

List of Figures and Tables

Figures

Tables

Acknowledgments

This book evolved from research done for a doctoral thesis in which evidence for the hypotheses was never discovered. The rejected hypothesis, that the black middle class had a weaker racial group identity than other blacks, hence more conservative political attitudes, led to an inquiry into the nature of racial group identity, and ultimately, this book. It could not have been completed, however, without the help of several people to whom I owe a debt of gratitude.

I must first thank the students whose words are the heart and soul of this book. I will always be grateful for their courage and openess. My dissertation adviser, Randall Strahan of Emory University, supported the research through every transformation. He read the initial draft, and contributed significantly to the organization of the manuscript. Toni Michelle-Travis provided extensive and detailed criticism of a later draft, and steered me to earlier works that became an essential part of the theoretical foundation for the book. Laura Stoker, in reading a final draft, helped me to focus more directly on the essential arguments, and rekindled my excitement about the story told by these students. Her detailed comments and editing were a godsend.

Jennifer Hochschild, whose work served as inspiration, gave me invaluable advice about maintaining an open mind about how young blacks might define labels such as "conservative" and "liberal," and what kinds of patterns of identity and ideology might be uncovered during the research. Maintaining this approach while conducting the interviews yielded information that was unexpected and intriguing. Michael Rogin suggested important changes in organization and additional material that helped clarify and illuminate ideological differences between the subjects. Carol Swain provided advice, career and otherwise, all along the way, and encouraged me to remain true to my subjects.

I want to thank Robert Crutchfield and the Institute for Ethnic Studies at the University of Washington for providing the funding to complete the interviews. My colleagues at the University of Washington, Michael McCann, Donald McCrone, Lance Bennett, Peter May, and especially Christine DiStefano, were among the first to respond enthusiastically to this project. John T. S. Keeler shared with me one of the best undergraduate research assistants around—Dan Valadez. University of Washington graduate students Bonnie Lyon, Valerie Hunt, and especially Norma Rodriguez did much of the library research and copying of articles. Others who offered valuable advice or whose work was essential to the development of the book are: Michael Dawson, Manley Elliot Banks, Katherine Tate, and Beth Reingold.

The staff and faculty at the six interview sites were enormously helpful. The required anonymity of the subjects and site locations prevents me from naming them here. These men and women not only agreed to serve as liaisons between the researcher, students, and the university, but went far beyond the call of duty by providing space for the interviews and parking privileges when needed. I will never forget your thoughtful consideration.

The book may not have been completed without the time afforded me by the University of California, Berkeley as a fellow in the Chancellor's Postdoctoral Program for Academic Diversity. A year in Michael Hout's spacious quarters at the Survey Research Center was enough to stimulate the dullest of minds. I thank Professor Hout for his generosity and for the use of his outstanding library. Fredrick Harris, my "postdoctoral partner in residence," engaged me in highly productive debates about identity and ideology among African-Americans. In sharing insights gleaned from his comparative work on black identity in Great Britain and South Africa, Professor Harris helped me to sort out explanations for some of my findings.

My editor, Niko Pfund, demonstrated unflagging faith in my work by his prompt, detailed, and incisive though tactful criticisms. I am grateful that my first publishing experience has been such a rewarding one. Finally, I want to thank my family—my mother, Clara M. Simpson; my sisters, Sandra Puckett, Dr. Patricia Terry, Beverly Simpson, and Rochelle Hills; my nieces, Tiffany, Alysia, and Kristen; my nephews, Edward and Everett; my brother, James Arthur Simpson, Jr.; and my stepchildren, Teddy and Genny Maloney, for their constant support. A special thanks is reserved for my husband, Alonzo, for his steadfast love and kindness. Although many contributed to this project, the responsibility for any errors is completely mine.

1

Introduction

This is a book about what it means to be black, specifically, what it means to be black to members of a generation who many hoped would never have to ponder such a question. It is also a book about how answers to this question influence this generation's political attitudes. The perspectives of the young men and women in this book are critically important as the debate about the political effectiveness of racial solidarity versus coalition-building rages on. Will race continue to be a powerful and effective determinate of political outcomes? Has integration allowed the post–civil rights generation to build a bridge across the racial chasm in this country? According to the members of the post–civil rights generation featured here, the power of race to divide communities, destroy friendships, and determine opportunity has not been diminished. Racial segregation continues in the midst of integrated institutions—parallel universes of black and white.

Occupants of the black universe are the subjects of this book, and their perspectives are the foundation of this portrait of post–civil rights experiences. Earlier works on race, class, and gender explored similar issues. E. Franklin Frazier (1939) described and analyzed the evolution of the black family in America, including the development of class divisions. Frazier explained how social conditions throughout history—slavery, rural life, and the great migration to northern cities—resulted in cultural adaptations that allowed African-Americans to construct stable societies. The present work, too, indicates that black people are still finding ways to adapt to social conditions that meet the human need for acceptance and validation.

The conditions, limitations, and opportunities of city blacks in the post–World War II era were studied by Drake and Cayton ([1945]

1962). Relationships with whites, discrimination, political attitudes, school integration, and the sharing of public spaces were the phenomena they analyzed. Much of what they found—mistrust of whites and discomfort around whites—will be found here.

Recent work by Feagin and Sikes (1994) on the black middle class describes the nature of discrimination faced by blacks who are in majority-white settings. Parents of small children speak about the lack of books by and about blacks in school libraries, and the reluctance of teachers and librarians to advocate inclusion of these books. Black college students talk about subtle and not-so-subtle humiliations suffered at the hands of white professors. Black professionals talk about being shut out of the informal social circles that can help pave the way to success. Feagin and Sikes focus on the *experience* of racism in a variety of arenas. This work extends that focus to include the relationship between the experience of racism, the development of black identity, and the formation of political attitudes.

Race remains highly effective as a political wedge. Yet at the same time, political liaisons based on shared racial group membership are being criticized from many different quarters. For example, the need for gerrymandered electoral districts to increase opportunities for black residents to elect black representatives has been judged unconstitutional in many states, which implies that representation of blacks need not mean black representatives.[1] What is really being contested here is the significance of racial group identity and the viability of a unique black experience. In other words, if serving an African-American constituency does not require any special knowledge or understanding about African-Americans as a group, it follows that African-Americans do not have any needs particular to their group. Anyone is capable of representing their interests.

A question around which much racial tension has accumulated of late is whether affirmative action is still necessary or justified. Are African-Americans so subjugated and disadvantaged as a group that extraordinary measures should be taken to ensure equal opportunity? If the decisions and behavior of the individual determine life chances and experiences, then racial policies should be abandoned. But if racial group membership, despite the decisions and behavior of the individual, does affect life chances and experiences, then racial policies remain necessary. Additionally, members of this group may indeed have a deeper comprehension of the social and political dynamics of the group, and may use this knowledge to better serve them. This is not to suggest that members of other groups are constitutionally incapable of serving a black constituency, only that the reality of black group identity makes black representation meaningful.

Despite strident commentary from whites and blacks on the destructiveness of race-based politics, major studies demonstrate that race remains salient for African-Americans and that most African-Americans retain solid racial identities.[2] One of the fundamental reasons cited for this phenomenon is the continuing economic inequality between whites and blacks, feeding the perception that widespread discrimination persists. Racially charged events such as the beating of Rodney King and revelations of continuing police brutality—as in the case of the Los Angeles and Philadelphia police departments—only reinforce this perception.

It is clear that individual blacks feel connected to other blacks, profoundly influencing political attitudes and behavior. The subjects of this book tell us that this feeling is not always one of collective fate. For example, some believe that their socioeconomic status and education insulates them from the problems of poorer and uneducated blacks, but obligates them to help solve those problems. Helping sometimes means voting for the party or policy that will benefit the poorest among the group. It can also mean tutoring or mentoring young people, or organizing community groups. In other words, some members of the "integration generation" would like to expand the definition of blackness beyond shared experiences of discrimination or a sense of collective fate. Glenn Loury has written that he is "more than the one wronged, misunderstood, underestimated, derided, or ignored by whites."[3] Desmond Apprey, one of the students you will meet here, sarcastically says, "What does it take to be black? Oh, is there a list we have? Black, OK, at one time you had to have kente cloth. See—I'm out."

What is the root cause of racial identity, in this case black identity? One of the young men interviewed here believes that the racist attitudes of whites force blacks to construct a black identity. This is what Du Bois (1903) meant by his lament that blacks are forced to see themselves through the eyes of others—as if through a veil. For Du Bois, and for some of the students here, the image is a negative one. Others believe that black identity is an inherent, fixed attribute. If black identity is constructed, what factors influence its manifestation? This book reveals how environment, class, and experiences with racism contribute to individual beliefs about what it means to *be black*.

The question of racial group identity leads to another, more politically significant, question about political attitudes regarding racial issues. If black identity has been weakened by integration, can the tradition of Democratic liberalism continue in the black community? Are blacks going to continue to be united on issues of affirmative action and civil rights? In recent years a number of black conservatives, espousing anti-affirmative action views and calling for a color-blind society, have emerged. Scholars have been unable to identify a significant constituency for these views in the black community. Yet there are two organizations of Young Republicans at historically black colleges. Could there be a conservative wave forming among members of the "integration generation"?

Developments on the Right

In the past several years, two kinds of African-American conservatives have achieved national prominence. One is a product of the Reagan-Bush era, a true believer in the free market, small government, and personal responsibility as the formula for the good life. The other kind is also a believer in the free market, less reliance on government (though not necessarily small government), personal responsibility, and is influenced by black nationalism. The latter kind of conservative also believes ardently in the conservation of African-American culture, which involves some separation, mainly social and economic, from the majority culture.

These two groups of conservatives have shared the spotlight in several compelling events and developments. First, the confirmation hearings on the nomination of Clarence Thomas to the Supreme Court in October 1991 paraded before the mass public many of those rarely seen, but much talked, about black conservative politicos of the Reagan-Bush era. These conservative blacks testified on behalf of Justice Thomas during the hearings that followed Anita Hill's accusations that Thomas had sexually harassed her during her tenure at the Department of Education's Commission on Civil Rights. They included men and women, many of whom held positions in the Bush administration, and others who had attended law school with Thomas. Their conservatism was apparent from their partisan affiliation (most were Republicans), as well as obvious indications that they shared many of Thomas's political views. What has often been overlooked in the valorization of Anita Hill is that she was essentially the same kind of conservative as Clarence Thomas.

In the wake of the hearings, publications critical of affirmative action by writers such as Shelby Steele and Stephen Carter have staked out important and controversial positions. Steele (1990) and Carter (1991) both wrote books arguing that affirmative action does more harm than good by saddling blacks with the stigma of inferiority. According to Kinder and Sanders (1996), white opposition to affirmative action in college admissions triggers opposition to other kinds of racial policies. This opposition comes from the perception of personal racial threat—that the blacks who are admitted may take the place of family members and friends who are more deserving. The animosity generated by affirmative action in college admissions may be part of what is driving the students here to conservatism—both black nationalist and Republican Party conservatism. Both brands of conservatism advocate self-help and individual responsibility. Sensitivity to anti-affirmative action sentiments can lead to different forks on the same road.

In October 1995, Louis Farrakhan, leader of the Nation of Islam, organized the "Million Man March" in Washington, D.C. The march, according to Farrakhan, was to atone for the failure of black men to care properly for their families and their communities. Adolph Reed has said that "as a friend of mine aptly noted, it was the first protest

in history where people gathered ostensibly to protest themselves"
(Reed 1995). This event attracted somewhere between 800,000 and 1.5
million men, and was televised on the Cable News Network (CNN)
in its entirety. Marchers came from all walks of life; the march cut
across socioeconomic strata, age, and region. It raised Farrakhan to a
new level of national prominence, and was a tangible demonstration
of the palliative power of Farrakhan's rhetoric.

These developments beg questions about how race is being transformed within the post–civil rights black community. What has contributed to the popularity of both kinds of conservatism? What role
has integration played in either of these movements? What are the
possible political outcomes of these phenomena?

The Black Solidarity Imperative

A conservative trend among African-Americans, at least on issues of
government spending and policies concerning racial equality, has yet
to be confirmed by systematic research (Tate 1994; Dawson 1994;
Gilliam 1986). African-Americans tend to be highly homogeneous
ideologically, with blacks voting overwhelmingly Democratic in presidential elections (Smith and Seltzer 1985:105; Asher 1988:82). This
trend has persisted through all modern presidential elections.

African-American political solidarity has persisted in part because
of the strength of racial group identity, or group consciousness. Research shows that black group consciousness is an important factor in
determining levels of participation (Verba and Nie 1972). African-
American group consciousness was a catalyst for the political activism of the 1960s and 1970s. Distinctions are sometimes made between group *identification* and group *consciousness* (Miller et al. 1981).
The former can be characterized as the objective classification of the
individual—the group to which a person can be assigned, or assigns
him- or herself, without subjective considerations. The latter is the
politicization of that identity—the awareness that the objective
group to which the individual belongs is denied certain benefits and
privileges by society, thereby denying the individual benefits. Con-

sciousness can also be defined as "feelings of closeness" to other blacks (Demo and Hughes 1990; Allen, Dawson, and Brown 1989; Gurin, Miller, and Gurin 1980). Extending these definitions to blacks in particular, it would be possible to feel kinship with blacks without feeling that systemic inequities are to blame for the status of blacks. Scholars in this field use both terms, "identity" and "consciousness," interchangeably. In this work, the term "identity" connotes feelings of closeness to other blacks *and* the degree to which respondents believe that society oppresses blacks as a group.

Assimilation and the Psychology of Nigrescence

We cannot discuss the salience of group identification without addressing assimilation. The goal of integration was not to eliminate the cultural identity of blacks, but to facilitate an understanding and acceptance of that identity. It has failed, and members of the post–civil rights generation are as race-conscious as previous generations. What is assimilation, and why has it been impossible for blacks to achieve? What keeps black identity so dynamic?

Assimilation is a concept that holds some negative connotations in contemporary thinking about race relations. Some think of assimilation as the obliteration of the culture of the minority in a fashion that denigrates the minority culture. One of the reasons that assimilation has been disparaged is that it is associated with the idea that ethnic groups, particularly African-Americans, have nothing of value to preserve in their own cultures. Assimilation is thus perceived as the abandonment of the core identity of the individual, and perhaps even more important, as a concession in the cold war for cultural dominance.

Others subscribe to the view that assimilation is the *incorporation* of the minority culture, which helps to form a hybrid culture. The hybrid culture, and ultimately the dominant culture, would be "American" culture. However, not only is "American" culture dominated by Anglo-American ideals, but African-Americans, Latinos, Native Americans, and Asian-Americans often find that the battle for acceptance continues in spite of efforts to fit in. The experience of individuals who have come to identify as completely American, only to realize that they are not in fact accepted as such, can result in the development of the "marginal man," caught between his ethnic group and the group with which he identifies.[4] It may also result, as we will see, in the development of an acute awareness of the importance of ethnic group membership.

Part of the current racial debate is about whether it is possible for minorities to maintain a separate and distinct subculture *and* achieve economic, political, and social equality. For many the ideal solution is to eliminate ignorance of, and prejudice against, minority groups through education. This way minority groups could preserve their history and folkways, yet enjoy a primary benefit of assimilation—the elimination of discrimination and full integration into the social fabric of the majority.

Integration into the social fabric of the majority requires that members of the minority develop primary relationships with members of the majority (Gordon 1964). Primary relationships are ones in which people interact on a personal basis. They share all aspects of their lives and spend leisure time together. Secondary relationships, on the other hand, are those in which people share only segments of their lives—work, or perhaps a hobby. These relationships are formal. Most relationships between blacks and whites are secondary ones. One of the reasons for this is that whether rich or poor, blacks remain residentially segregated. In fact, if more than a few African-American families move into an all-white neighborhood, the neighborhood rapidly "turns over," with black families replacing the white families that move out (Massey and Denton 1993). Residential segregation is perpetuated by institutionalized racism, which denies home mortgages to blacks in certain areas.

Primary relationships can develop through interracial marriages, which have dramatically increased since miscegenation laws were lifted in 1967. In 1960, only about 2 percent of all African-American marriages included a white partner. By 1990 the figure had increased to 6 percent. However, a few moments on the worldwide web will yield numerous sites on interracial relationships, many of which point out the religious and social dictates against interracial dating and marriage, especially between African-Americans and whites. One of the young women interviewed here, Laura Womack, poignantly describes how her Japanese mother's admonitions not to act "black" affected her and her siblings. Interracial marriages are not an automatic solution to racial prejudice.

African-Americans have not been assimilated largely because of continuing discrimination. While blacks have been in this country as long as whites and do not face the language barriers confronting other minority groups,[5] they are distinguished by a history of enslavement in this country. The institution of slavery, justified by the notion that blacks were subhuman, also propagated various other negative stereotypes regarding blacks. These stereotypes linger today, and are part of the reason discrimination continues. While European minority groups were also stereotyped, once accents were dropped and names were changed, ethnic origins became impossible to detect. Eventually, stereotypes associated with these groups vanished. Blacks have not been able to conceal their racial group membership, and the stereotyping of blacks continues to be a problem.

There is a strange dichotomy in the failure of blacks to assimilate. On the one hand, African-Americans can be considered more "American" than most groups, since they have contributed significantly to American cultural identity through art and politics. Stanley Crouch writes that the significance of leaders such as Frederick Douglass and Rosa Parks extends far beyond their "blackness," as was witnessed when "We Shall Overcome" appeared on a placard during the protest in Tiananmen Square.[6] On the other hand, as these students remind us, claiming an "American" identity is difficult in the face of continuing racial inequality.

How does black identity develop? Literature on the psychology of nigrescence (the process of becoming black), posits that there are five stages in this process: pre-encounter; encounter; immersion-emersion; internalization; and internalization-commitment (Cross 1991:190). A lack of knowledge about one's race, and sometimes antiblack feelings, characterize the pre-encounter stage. The encounter stage, which is of particular interest in this work, and may be positive or negative, sudden or gradual, is characterized by the dawning of racial group awareness. Students who came to this understanding abruptly seem to more firmly embrace the third stage of nigrescence, immersion, which is marked by an obsession with blackness. This may be followed by the emersion stage, which is a leveling-off of the obsessive stage and the beginning of the internalization stage. A commitment to black interests may or may not follow the internalization of black identity (Cross 1991:200–20). Individuals do not always proceed from one stage to the next in an orderly fashion. They may regress to the pre-encounter stage during the immersion-emersion stage, or be catapulted back into the immersion stage during the internalization stage.

Integration at an early age seems to encourage weak group identity among African-Americans (Demo and Hughes 1990; Thompson 1991). If racial group identity is indeed weakened by early interaction with whites, what can we expect to happen as the generation that has experienced the most intense integration efforts in American history comes to political maturity? Will we see more multiracial political coalitions? Will the Democratic Party lose its stronghold on the black voting bloc? Or has integration fostered increased racial hostility?

These questions cannot be answered now, but the students in this book give us a preview of what is possible. Integration was supposed to foster understanding through the development of friendships. The reality of integration falls far short of this ideal. In fact, after years of court-ordered busing and the ardent pursuit of blacks by colleges and universities, schools at the elementary and secondary levels are becoming resegregated.[7] Colleges and universities are embroiled in conflict over the booking of speakers such as Khalid Muhammed, the former youth minister of the Nation of Islam, and ethnic organizations flourish.

Class and Race

Students in this book talk about their disappointment in the stereotype of blacks as poor. In their view, the stereotype is powerful enough to convince whites and blacks that having an authentic black✓ identity entails coming from an impoverished background. For some of them, this particular stereotype makes them reluctant to accept that there are any specific points of commonality among blacks. The middle- to upper-class students have been protected from some of the more virulent racism witnessed by the poorer students, so there is little doubt that socioeconomic status in this generation has made a difference in the way that these students experience the world. More-over, they have had opportunities to develop interests that do not fit conventional beliefs about African-American life. Therefore these students have different concepts of blackness, but most agree that being black still affects their lives.

The argument surrounding the question of whether race or class is most significant in determining the life chances of individuals seems unresolvable because there has been progress, relapse, and stagnation in the struggle for racial equality. If we look at three measures of socioeconomic status—occupation, education, and income—from 1960 to 1994, it is clear that African-Americans have certainly made some progress since 1960. There has also been an

Figure 1.1. African-American Occupational Status (As a Percent of All Workers)

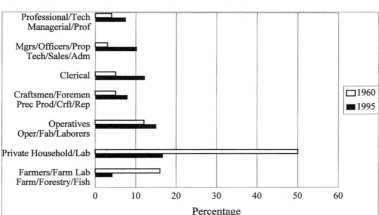

SOURCE: U.S. Bureau of the Census, *Statistical Abstract of the United States: 1996* (116th edition) Washington, DC, 1996. Current Population Reports, P23–28, Table 49.

Figure 1.2. African-American Occupational Status—Change in Percentage-Service Occupations

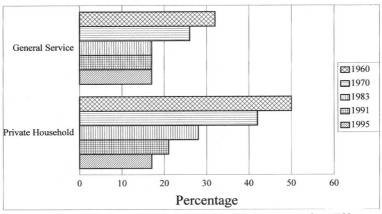

SOURCE: U.S Bureau of the Census, *Statistical Abstract of the United States: 1993 and 1996*, Tables 49 and 637. Current Population Reports P23–38, Table 49.

alarming lack of progress in some areas. In terms of occupation, an increase from 7 percent in 1960 to 18 percent in 1995 of African-Americans (as a percentage of total employed) in the highest two categories of employment—professional/technical/managerial and technical/sales/administrators—indicates that some African-Americans have been able to take advantage of opportunities in these areas. [See Figure 1.1] Although comparisons from 1960 to 1995 are difficult to make due to differences in the Census Bureau's occupational definitions, by combining some of the categories that have been rearranged, we can make a ballpark estimate of the percentage increase in these top professions. The bar charts in this chapter were carefully composed to match occupations as closely as possible, especially when comparing data from 1960 with subsequent years. One way of determining progress is to examine categories in which large numbers of African-Americans have been employed in the past, such as private household service jobs. [See Figure 1.2.] We can see that these percentages have declined from 50 percent in 1960 to less than 20 percent in 1995.

Black businesses have increased over 300 percent since 1972, with revenues soaring from $6 billion in 1972 to over $32 billion in 1992. These data are solid evidence of a thriving entrepreneurial spirit among African-Americans, and of a climate that is increasingly favorable to African-American business ventures.

But compare the progress of blacks in terms of occupational status and black business growth with progress in education. African-Americans remain dismally behind whites in college and postgraduate training, and have made little progress in almost forty years. In 1960, only 3 percent of African-Americans had four years of college or more. That figure increased to 13 percent by 1995—an increase of 10 percent. The percentage of whites increased by 16 percent—from 8 to 24 percent. The progress made in acquiring at least a high school diploma is considerable, but blacks will have to acquire more education in order to earn more money. Thirty percent of African-Americans with a college degree and postgraduate education earn more than twice the median income.

The data on income complete this portrait of black progress and

Figure 1.3. African-American Business Growth

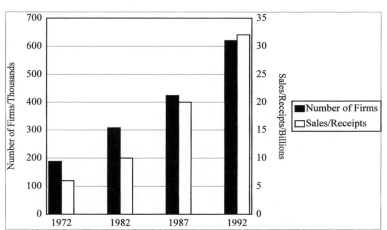

SOURCE: U.S. Department of Commerce, 1977, 1987. Table 841, U.S. Bureau of the Census, *Statistical Abstract of the United States: 1996* (116th edition), Washington, DC, 1996.

Figure 1.4. Educational Attainment, Blacks and Whites, 1960–1995

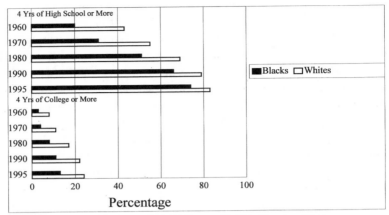

SOURCE: U.S. Bureau of the Census, *Statistical Abstract of the United States: 1996*, Table 241.

stagnation, and show that the poorest African-American households, those making $15,000 or less annually, have hovered around 35 percent for the past twenty years. [See Figure 1.5] The two highest income categories, blacks making $50,000 to $75,000 or more, have increased from about 10 percent to 17 percent.

Taken as a whole, these data indicate that a middle-class black America has emerged. Moreover, there is a great disparity between the black middle class and the black poor. This disparity is more meaningful than simple differences in income or occupation. These differences are clearly related to family structure as well, which may create cultural as well as economic barriers between the middle class and the poor. These figures give us only part of the story. The rest of the story is to be found in the tremendous change in the way African-Americans are educated, how they live, with whom they associate, and the conditions under which they work.

The 1970s and 1980s brought an increase in the number of African-Americans having to interact with whites on a more equal basis than in past years. Antidiscrimination laws give African-Americans some recourse when encountering poor treatment on the job, and whites

Figure 1.5. Household Income, Blacks and Whites, 1970–1994 (in Constant 1994 Dollars)

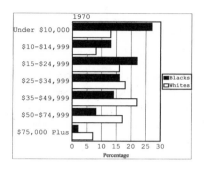

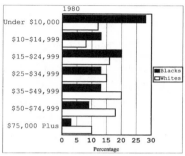

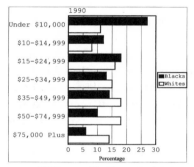

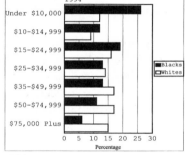

SOURCE: U.S Bureau of the Census, *Statistical Abstract of the United States: 1996*, Table 709.

have been made more aware of the existence and nature of discrimination. The social condition of African-Americans is vastly different in the 1990s. Poverty remains, although altered in its form by the use and sale of illegal drugs, the deterioration of the inner cities where most African-Americans live, and by the increasing numbers of female-headed, single-parent families. African-Americans and whites no longer automatically interact according to the unspoken rule that African-Americans are unable to hold a superior position to whites in the workplace. These differences in the ground rules which governed African-American and white relations in the past are one of the reasons some African-Americans may view issues of race from a more individual perspective.

Black Unity: Spanning the Generation Gap

None of the young people interviewed here were made to sit on the back of the bus or experience any other aspect of the segregated South. Many have attended the finest preparatory schools and traveled extensively around the world. As expected, some have parents who benefited from the gains of the civil rights movement, and who then gave their children opportunities and advantages they themselves had been denied. Therefore, we would expect these young people to have significantly different attitudes from those who have experienced both segregation and the denial of opportunities.

Two surveys, the National Black Politics Study (Dawson and Brown 1993) and the author's own survey of elites listed in *Who's Who among African Americans*, show that regardless of socioeconomic status, age, or gender, blacks believe that their individual fate is tied to the fate of the group. The former survey (hereafter called the NBPS), reflects the opinions of a broad spectrum of African-Americans, a third of whom would be considered middle class. The latter survey, the Elite Survey, represents the opinions of a small sample of middle- to upper-middle and upper-class African-Americans, all of whom are members of the civil rights generation.

A comparison of these two surveys is revealing in several ways. The two sample groups clearly illustrate the complexity of ideological perspectives among African-Americans. Both intergroup and intragroup comparisons reveal a significant degree of overall ideological homogeneity, particularly on affirmative action. However, on several issues measured in the NBPS, members of the post-civil rights generation are more pessimistic and separatist than members of the civil rights generation.

The National Black Politics Study (NBPS)

Two samples were extracted from the 1993–94 National Black Politics Study, a survey of twelve hundred respondents. One sample, the civil rights generation sample, contains respondents born between 1943 and 1958, so that these individuals would have been at crucial stages in the development of their political attitudes during the peak years of the civil rights movement and the black power movement. For example, those born in 1943 were eleven to thirteen years old during the Montgomery Bus Boycott and twenty-five years old by 1968, the year King was assassinated. Those born in 1958 were ten years old in 1968, but fourteen years old in 1972, during the years of the failed escape of Jonathan and George Jackson (the Soledad Brothers), which prompted an international manhunt for Angela Davis.[8]

The second sample, the post–civil rights generation, contains respondents born between 1959 and 1975. Individuals in this group were in the early stages of political socialization after the civil rights movement and during the decline of the black power movement. The civil rights generation cohort includes 385 respondents; the post–civil rights generation cohort includes 399 respondents. Women outnumber men in both samples: the civil rights generation has 131 men and 254 women, and the post–civil rights group has 158 men and 241 women. Each sample contains roughly the same number of Democrats and Republicans, and is comparable socioeconomically. Measures taken from this study are those on black identity, or the degree to which respondents feel that their fate is linked to the fate of other blacks; affirmative action; black nationalism; black progress toward racial equality; and gender issues.

As Figure 1.6 shows, these two generational cohorts show few differences on measures of black identity. Only about one in five of each group feels that what happens to other blacks will not affect him or her at all. Most of the respondents in each group believe that what happens to other blacks will affect them some, or a lot. The same is true for affirmative action. Figure 1.7 shows the responses to two questions regarding affirmative action. As this figure shows,

Figure 1.6. A Generational Comparison of Responses on Identity Question

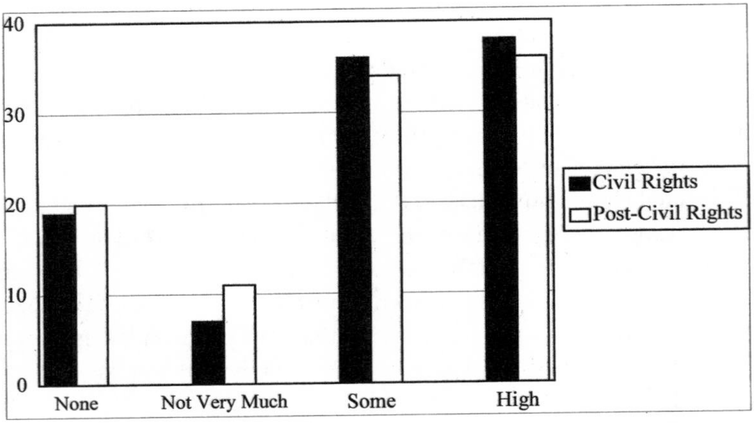

Do you think that what happens generally to black people in this country will have something to do with what happens in your life? Will it affect you a lot, some, or not very much?

SOURCE: National Black Politics Study, 1993–94. Principal Investigators: Ronald Brown, Wayne State University and Michael C. Dawson, University of Chicago.

most people in both groups express support for affirmative action, though somewhat less so when responding to the second question (approximately 65 percent) than to the first (approximately 90 percent).

Figure 1.8 shows how both groups respond to questions about economic versus political empowerment and the formation of a black political party. The post-civil rights generation is more concerned about coupling political empowerment strategies with economic empowerment strategies. More than half of this group supports the formation of a black political party.

Figure 1.9 shows additional differences regarding a measure of attitudes on gender discrimination. Well over half in the post–civil rights generation believe that black women suffer from sexism and racism, compared with slightly more than half of the civil rights generation. Conversely, a smaller percentage of the post–civil rights generation believes that black women suffer from the same problems as black men.

Small but interesting contrasts exist between the two groups about

Figure 1.7. A Generational Comparison of Responses on Affirmative Action

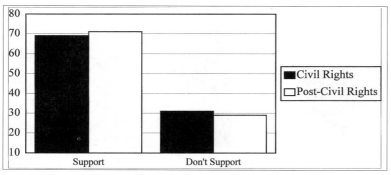

Please tell me which choice is most true for you:

There has been so much racial progress over the past several years that special programs for blacks are no longer needed.

There is still so much discrimination that special programs to help blacks and minorities are still needed.

Some people say that because of past discrimination blacks should be given preference in hiring and promotion. Others say that such preference in hiring and promotion is wrong because it give blacks advantages they haven't earned. What about your opinion—do you strongly agree, somewhat agree, somewhat disagree, or strongly disagree with preferential hiring and promotion of blacks?

SOURCE: National Black Politics Study, 1993–94. Prinicipal Investigators: Ronald Brown, Wayne State University and Michael C. Dawson, University of Chicago.

progress toward racial equality. Slightly less than half of the civil rights generation do not believe that blacks will achieve racial equality in their lifetime, while a little more than a third of the post–civil rights generation does, which makes sense since the civil rights gen-

Figure 1.8. A Generational Comparison of Responses on Economic and Political Empowerment and the Formation of a Black Political Party

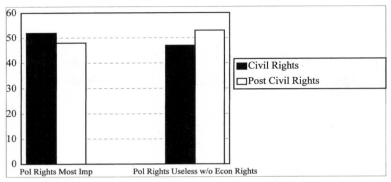

Please tell me which choice is more true for you:

Gaining political rights such as the vote has been most important for black progress.

Political rights, such as the vote, are useless unless economic rights are gained at the same time.

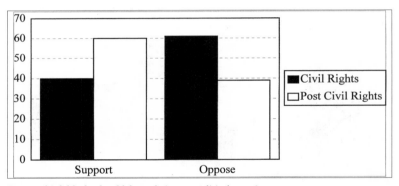

Do you think blacks should form their own political party?

SOURCE: National Black Politics Study, 1993–94. Principal Investigators: Ronald Brown, Wayne State University and Michael C. Dawson, University of Chicago.

eration has fewer years left than the post–civil rights generation. On the other hand, a fourth of the post–civil rights generation feel that blacks will never achieve racial equality, compared with only a fifth of the civil rights generation.

So, while there are generational differences on a few issues regarding gender considerations and the possibility of racial equality, over-

Figure 1.9. A Generational Comparison of Responses on
Race/Gender Question

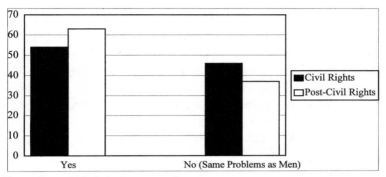

Please tell me which choice is most true for you:
Black women have suffered from both sexism within the black movement and racism within the women's movement.
Black women mostly suffer from the same problems as black men.

SOURCE: National Black Politics Study, 1993–94. Prinicipal Investigators: Ronald Brown, Wayne State University and Michael C. Dawson, University of Chicago.

Figure 1.10. A Generational Comparison of Responses on
Racial Optimism

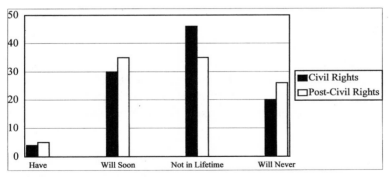

Do you think blacks have achieved racial equality, will soon achieve racial equality, will not achieve racial equality in your lifetime, will never achieve racial equality.

SOURCE: National Black Politics Study, 1993–94. Principal Investigators: Ronald Brown, Wayne State University and Michael C. Dawson, University of Chicago.

all these two generations are of one mind on racial issues. On the question of hope for racial equality, the post–civil rights group seems a bit more pessimistic than the civil rights group. A wealth of literature, from Cornel West (1993) to Nathan McCall (1995), speaks to the hopelessness and frustration of the post–civil rights generation. A 1996 *Newsweek* cover story on the black generation gap emphasized the different perspectives of the two generations on the appropriate way to achieve success in a racist society. The civil rights generation perceives more opportunities than ever, while the younger generation perceives fewer (Leland and Samuels 1996).

One might have expected more differences between these two groups on racial issues. The post–civil rights generation responds in the same way as the civil rights generation to most of the measures. We know that the post–civil rights generation has not had the same life experiences regarding race as the civil rights generation. To what may we attribute the absence of differences among these two groups? The young people in this book give us part of the answer. The post–civil rights generation, the "integration generation," may not have had the same experiences, but they have come face-to-face with a different kind of racism, one that is more subtle but just as powerful.

The Elite Survey

This survey of African-American elites is based on a random sample of 257 persons listed in *Who's Who among Black Americans* (1992).[9] Questions on black identity and affirmative action were taken from the National Black Election Study (Jackson 1993), and were worded as follows:

Black Identity:

People differ in whether they think about being black—what they have in common with other blacks. What about you—do you think about this a lot, fairly often, once in a while, or hardly ever?

Do you think what happens generally to black people in this country has anything to do with what happens in your life? If yes: will it affect you a lot, some, or not very much?

Affirmative Action:

Because of past discrimination, minorities should be given special consideration when decisions are made about hiring applicants for jobs. (Agree/Disagree)

    Job applicants should be judged solely on the basis of test scores and other individual qualities. (Agree/Disagree)

Blacks in this survey have a strong sense of linked fate with other blacks. Over half of these respondents think about being black a lot or fairly often, and almost three-fourths believe that what happens to other blacks will affect them, and of that group, two-fifths believe it will affect them a lot.

Affirmative action has become one of the main divisions between African-American conservatives and the rest of the community. The responses here indicate the complexities of these issues, especially among the recipients of these efforts. More than 40 percent of these respondents believe test scores should be the sole criterion for employment; however, approximately eight out of ten favor affirmative action. Contrasting their answers on affirmative action with their responses on job applicant test scores, we find an illustration of their attempt to reconcile the demands of racial progress and equal opportunity. Overall, these respondents are liberal on most issues, especially on affirmative action and the obligation of government to help minorities. This is confirmed by the fact that 88 percent registered disagreement with the statement "the government should not make any special effort to help blacks and other minorities because they should help themselves."

Finally, on the question of whether or not blacks will ever achieve full social and economic equality, nearly half of these respondents reply negatively, and about a third respond that they do not know. Comments written in the margins and on the backs of the Elite surveys served to explain many answers. They revealed an acute awareness of the problem of race in America, and are similar to some of the comments made by the students. A gentleman from the South wrote the following in response to an innocuous question about where he grew up: "One white woman, Daisy Packer, lived in the next block from me. Her husband was a drunkard and her parrot called us 'niggers.' We were forbidden to play ball or to skate in front of her house—she would call the cops." As he was an older man, the incident had remained vivid in his memory for a long time. This respondent also commented on whether government should make a special effort to help blacks and other minorities, writing: "The evils of racial discrimination are still with us."

While many answered that they lived in mostly white neighborhoods, had one or two white friends, and trusted "some" white people (many wrote in the margin that they also trusted only "some" black people)—all moderate responses—other responses showed that they were pessimistic about race relations and the opportunities for African-Americans. A middle-aged affirmative action administrator in the Northeast, who answered moderately on questions of interaction with, and trust of whites, responded as follows to the question about whether blacks would ever achieve full social and economic equality: "No. Racism is ingrained in our social and economic and educational institutions."

Questions on affirmative action and test scores as a criterion for employment also inspired extensive comments. A retired teacher in the North wrote on the subject of test scores: "This only works in the military. Almost always, whites are given preference in the real world. Whites do not reject the many advantages they are heir to directly because of the long history of racism, do they?" A northern judge wrote that blacks can achieve success only "if arbitrary obstacles are not placed in their way. But like the glass ceiling in corporate America, some segments of society only want us to go so far, even if we have the skills and talent to go to the top."

African-Americans in the Elite Survey were certain about the need for affirmative action programs and government help for minorities because they were certain about continuing racial discrimination. African-Americans share a history, traditions, religion, and other aspects of cultural life, but current life experiences—of exclusion, stifled careers, frustrating workplaces—are also shared. The discrimination experienced by a maintenance worker may be blatant and coarse. The discrimination experienced by a university professor may be concealed and civilized, but the essence of both experiences is the same. These life experiences have helped shape the homogeneous political attitudes of African-Americans. As Ellis Cose wrote in the insightful *Rage of a Privileged Class*, "the often hurtful and seemingly trivial encounters of daily existence are in the end what most of life is" (Cose 1993:192). If this statement is true, then the significance of race in shaping political attitudes is not difficult to understand.

The Integration Generation, Racial Group Identity, and Political Attitudes

Michael Dawson has convincingly argued that racial group identity serves as a proxy for determining individual benefits or life chances. How strong this identity is depends on the availability of information about the African-American political, social, and economic worlds and the personal salience of racial group membership (Dawson 1994:11). Residential, educational, or social isolation of individual blacks from other blacks would then be one way in which this information could be truncated. If this isolation is combined with a perception that racial group identity has little meaning in one's personal life, this identity is weakened. How do individuals process information about the political, social, and economic worlds of blacks when they are isolated from other blacks during part of their lives, or exist in both a majority and a minority environment? What about those who experience a combination of race, gender, and class discrimination? What about those reared in rural environments as opposed to urban environments?

My research shows that integration may serve to weaken group identity in some individuals, but when combined with other factors such as socioeconomic background, gender, and an urban perspective, integration may serve to strengthen racial group identity. African-American student leaders in these pages indicate that the strength and power of group identity are contextual in part, meaning that it takes on different characteristics depending on whether the environment is majority black or majority white. Identical levels of identity animate a variety of political attitudes, from radical to conservative, which reveals that racial group identity is fluid. Racial identity is not a fixed state—it interacts with other elements, and may change in intensity as these elements recede or advance in relevance. High levels of group identity may combine with other factors such as low socioeconomic status, experiences with or exposure to racial discrimination, and urban environments to produce black nationalist tendencies. Weak group identity, combined with other factors such as middle or upper socioeconomic status, few or no experiences with racial discrimination, and rural environments may produce a more traditional conservative ideology.

Four distinct themes emerge from these interviews: first, black nationalist conservatism is reconcilable with Republican Party conservatism. Second, a minority group environment (whether or not African-Americans are in the majority or in the minority) may affect the strength of group identity and political attitudes. Third, rural environments may encourage more traditional conservatism than urban environments. Fourth, gender issues may begin to command equal time with race issues. Out of thirteen women interviewed, only two were traditional conservatives in their political attitudes, and none were conservative-nationalists, which suggests that the intersection of racial group identity and political attitudes may develop differently among women. Other factors, such as experiences with racism and the respondents' memories of their first awareness of racial differences, are crucial in the processing of the meaning of race in the students' individual lives and in the lives of others.

Group identity remains a potent force in the lives of young African-Americans. More important, black students at predominantly white universities seem acutely aware of the importance of race in their lives. Why? Perhaps because their efforts to become a part of these institutions have largely been unsuccessful. Black students are present in these places of prestige and privilege, but not embraced by them. This failure of blacks to become an integrated part of larger society has led to a strengthening of group identity and the elevation of black nationalist sentiments.

Historically, attempts to organize and mobilize blacks have emphasized their unique history and culture in order to articulate a black identity (Omi and Winant 1994). Marcus Garvey and the "Back to Africa" movement gave us the red, black, and green colors of liberation revived by the Black Power Movement in the 1960s. Garvey and his followers implicitly anticipated the Black Power Movement's mantra, "Black is beautiful." However, in the 1960s, the politicization of black identity was more successful than it had been in the past. While Garvey struggled for support, the movement that began with King and ended with the Black Panther Party was embraced by most African-Americans.

The idea behind the "Black is beautiful" era of the 1960s was to rid blacks of shame over skin color, hair texture, and facial and body features. The adoption of things African was meant not only to unify them, but also to help prepare them for integration—when their difference might become a source of ignominy. This strategy has broken down in the formidable face of integration, leading to frustration and a strengthening of black identity.

A Look Ahead

Due to the sensitive nature of this research, the names of both the students and the institutions have been kept confidential. The interviews took place in three historically black and three majority-white institutions. In an effort to aid the reader in understanding references to institutions and subjects that appear throughout the text, the fictitious names of the historically black institutions begin with "B," and the names of majority-white institutions with "W." Conservative students' first names begin with "C," moderate students with "M," and liberal students with "L." (Please refer to Appendix A for a detailed account of the research methods and background on interview subjects.)

The next chapter illustrates the ideological freedom experienced by students in a majority-black institution. All members of the campus-sponsored Young Black Republicans, these young men feel liberated from the obligation that blacks in integrated situations feel to demonstrate ideological unity. In the third chapter, students show how identity may be influenced as much by regional mores and cultural norms as race. This mostly southern and rural group was more ambivalent about affirmative action and more supportive of welfare reform. The moderate students in the fourth chapter cast a critical eye in the direction of whites and blacks when assessing the reasons for racial conflict, while the liberals in chapter five are inclined to blame white racism. Women in this group are becoming aware of the added burden of gender in their lives, and are groping for ways to incorporate both race and gender in their political activities. The sixth and final chapter reveals patterns of responses that affirm the heterogeneity and homogeneity of black political attitudes. Students' responses on Farrakhan, experiences with racism, and black leadership are surprisingly similar—their opinions on the black media are dissimilar. In the following chapters, the perspectives of two dozen intelligent and articulate college students convey how their identities and attitudes have been formed in a social and political environment of hope and rejection, breakthroughs and rollbacks.

2

The Conservatives, Part 1
The Republican Race Men

The most dynamic leaders in the African-American community have emerged from historically black institutions—Martin Luther King, Jr., Andrew Young, and Maynard Jackson (Morehouse College), to name a few. All the students featured in this chapter are attending two of the three historically black institutions selected for this research: Brooks College and Barnett University. Historically black colleges and universities have proven to be fertile ground for those who would seek to change conditions of poverty and neglect in the black community. Their tactics and strategies for change have ranged from political mobilization and legal challenges to nonviolent protest. The first two methods are clearly within the traditional boundaries of the democratic process. The latter approach, while considered radical in its day, especially in comparison to legal battles waged by organizations such as the NAACP, seems less radical today. The aim of the nonviolent protest movement of the 1960s was to force those in power to apply the law of the land equally to both blacks and whites. In other words, the leaders created by these institutions, whether committed to legal strategies or nonviolent protest, were committed to the ideals of a pluralist democracy. Leaders in the black community who would embrace black nationalism have not come from these institutions in the past. However, that may be changing. The "integration generation" is incorporating black nationalist ideas into more traditional approaches to social and political change. The conservatism demonstrated by some of the young people in this chapter is quite different from the more public black conservatives of the civil rights generation. Before these students speak for themselves, let us revisit the ideas espoused by the established black conservative leadership.

Contemporary Issues—Individualism, Responsibility, and Racism

The work of several contemporary conservatives, particularly economists Thomas Sowell (1984), Walter Williams (1982, 1987), and Glenn Loury (1984, 1987a, b), advances the following themes: (1) individual responsibility for one's own welfare; (2) the inability of government to solve most of the problems facing the black community; and (3) the importance of factors other than racism (such as education) in determining the success of African-Americans. Glenn Loury, unlike the other two economists, puts an emphasis on moral traditionalism. These scholars argue that government intervention in the economy, the sponsorship of affirmative action, and the legislation of a minimum wage are not helpful for blacks or other people. Related to their view of government intervention is their criticism of politicians who blame institutional racism as the root of black poverty. They believe solutions can only be found if black leaders face the facts as they find them—that internal problems such as antisocial behavior, lack of discipline, teen pregnancies, and failure in schools are the reasons for these conditions. In their view, dependence on government solutions to these problems only guarantees that the problems will become more intractable.

Shelby Steele (1990) and Stephen Carter (1991), both academics, also argue against affirmative action as a way for African-Americans to gain access to mainstream America. They recognize the existence of racism, but see it as less important than individual commitment to achievement. For Shelby Steele, racism is not the roadblock to success that it once was in this country. The psychological hold that racism has on blacks is the real roadblock. Stephen Carter wants African-Americans to be the best, not just the "best black." He believes affirmative action encourages the latter, not the former. Carter also believes that the existence of affirmative action causes those in power to generalize from the aggregate to the individual, but not the reverse. In other words, there is a definition of what "black" is, and what is possible for the "typical black." When an exceptional person is encountered, if he or she happens to be black, it is assumed that this person is an "exceptional black." Carter and Steele do not have prescriptions for mass political mobilization or thoughts about solutions to welfare, but their work on affirmative action has contributed significantly to the overall debate on the salience of racism in African-American life.

Stanley Crouch (1990, 1993), Robert Woodson (1992), and Alan Keyes (1989, 1993), distinct in the positions they occupy in public life, are also independent in terms of their conservative ideology. Stanley Crouch is a jazz critic and political essayist; Robert Woodson is a community organizer and activist; and Alan Keyes is a politician. All agree that issues of responsibility for one's own welfare supersede issues of racism. However, Alan Keyes and Stanley Crouch advance ideas for political empowerment that are not shared by Robert Woodson. Alan Keyes wants African-Americans to think independently and stop voting en masse for Democratic candidates. He believes that issue-voting must become more important than voting based on race. Stanley Crouch believes the politics of the practical—coalition-building, deal-making, and compromising—must replace politics that divide and exploit white guilt. Keyes and Crouch want less dependence on government and more individual responsibility, but they seek political means to those ends.

Woodson's ideas for economic empowerment are in the tradition of Booker T. Washington. He wants African-Americans to concentrate less on electoral politics and more on economic strategies through increased entrepreneurship. Woodson and Keyes agree on less government intervention in that they both advocate tenant involvement and eventual ownership of public housing. These two independent thinkers agree on the need for adherence to moral traditionalism within the black community by strengthening the church as an institution.

The question of who is responsible for the situation of African-

Americans is answered differently by these political thinkers. Sowell, Williams, Woodson, and Keyes believe that government social programs are responsible, along with an erosion of morality. Loury says that it does not matter who is responsible for the despair; all that matters is that blacks themselves must work to alleviate it.

Solutions to the problems proposed by these intellectuals and activists involve efforts to motivate blacks to acquire more education, postpone having children, abandon long-term welfare dependence, and practice new political strategies that include less allegience to the Democratic Party and more coalition-building. The best way to do this, according to some of the authors, is through private organizations, the church, and the mentoring of young blacks by older blacks who have been successful.

The young black conservatives interviewed here do not disagree with these tenets. However, they are clearly committed to the notion that race is an important factor in the lives of African-Americans. Some are all for coalition-building, but their focus is on intraracial rather than interracial coalitions. They are the "race men" of their generation, and offer a unique perspective on solutions to problems in the black community.

The Black Nationalist Conservatives

Clifford Apprey and Charles Gaston—Brooks College

Historically black colleges have catered to the children of the black middle class. In the past, nationalism has attracted more individuals from the working and lower classes than from the middle class. Some aspects of nationalist ideology are compatible with the traditional conservatism of the Republican Party. This combination of Republican and black nationalist conservatism is in evidence at Brooks and Barnett.

The four students interviewed at these institutions are active in the Republican Party. They were asked to volunteer because they self-identified as conservative and Republican. All were integrated at early ages and attended mostly majority-white and academically challenging high schools.

Two of the students interviewed, Clifford Apprey and Charles Gaston, have been working hard in the Republican Party at the local and state levels for several years. Both are from upper-middle-class, two-parent households with strong father figures. Neither of their mothers are employed outside the home, and both their fathers are professionals. Clifford Apprey's parents are from Africa, and his father lives and works in the United States. Clifford looks to this father for political guidance, and admires his father's drive and independence. Charles Gaston's parents are from the West Indies, and his father's political views, as a new immigrant, were shaped by optimism about his chances for prosperity.

Clifford and Charles are both pleased with their choice of a historically black college, as neither had ever spent time in majority-black environments at school. The history and culture of the college infuse these young men with race pride, as well as loyalty to the legacy left by previous graduates. However, the formation of a Young Republican organization is a new development at historically black colleges, and is at odds with the prevailing ideology at such institutions. Black Republicans are much harder to find at majority-white institutions, which was initially puzzling. However, Clifford Apprey explained why he and his friends felt freer to establish such an organization at Brooks than they would at a majority-white institution:

> A lot of times it's two or three blacks, or twenty blacks . . . [and] we couldn't say that you and I disagree because to lose them is to lose half my arm. So, you say "I agree with Charles." But you don't really agree with Charles, you just can't afford not to agree with Charles. . . . That's the great thing about going to African-American institutions. You're allowed to forge your own identity.

In other words, Clifford asserts that there is no compelling reason to present a unified front. This implies that it is more important to preserve racial unity in a majority-white environment than when in a majority-black environment.

For example, one of the students at Woodson University, a majority-white institution, mentioned that her decision to attend Woodson rather than a historically black college in the area was based on the feeling that the black students at Woodson were more "together." The black students at the historically black college seemed unconcerned, in her view, about black issues.

There is another factor that may contribute to the emphasis on black unity on majority-white campuses. Many leading black nationalist writers and scholars are now professors at majority-white institutions (Lemann 1993:34). Such scholars are helping to mold the opinions of black students. Accordingly, "A black college student's nationalism can be divided in half: part of it is a working out of one's relationship with black America, and part is the working out of one's relationship with white America" (Lemann 1993:43). In interviews with students at Temple University and the University of Pennsylvania, Lemann discovered African-American students who planned to live and work with whites, while using their skills and knowledge to help blacks in poor communities.

Some scholars argue that there is a generation gap developing in the black community that separates the pre–civil rights generation from the post–civil rights generation. Young African-American students have come of age under the political administrations of Reagan and Bush; they have thus experienced or witnessed few political victories on the part of minority leaders (Marable and Mullings 1994). Combined with other factors, this makes black nationalism attractive to this generation. The "hip-hop"[1] generation, which is the generation born after 1964, has little reason to expect to become a part of mainstream America. These youth have witnessed the emergence of poverty that resists amelioration; an increase in homelessness; and the continued brutality of law enforcement officials. These circumstances give them little hope for the future, making immediate gratification an integral part of the "hip-hop" culture.

Cornel West asserts that it is the hopelessness of the "hip-hop" generation that spawned the hero worship of Malcolm X. He refers to Malcolm X as the "prophet of rage"—a figure who articulated, in his manner and words, the frustration and anger of African-American youth (West 1993). West agrees with Marable and Mullings that this generation feels alienated from American society. This alienation encourages them to seek stronger kinship ties with Africa. The Afrocentric movement in higher education serves this need, and further promotes a nationalist outlook.

Studies indicate that blacks who interact with whites prior to adulthood are not attracted to nationalism, nor do they feel close to other blacks. The amount of contact with whites in adulthood is negatively related to black separatism (Demo and Hughes 1990:371). In other words, whether one is in the pre-adult or adult phase of development, increased interaction with whites weakens racial group identity. However, this research shows that while this may be true in part, a change in environment may trigger new interest in racial group identity.

This is illustrated by the experiences of Charles Gaston. Charles is an imposing young man both physically and intellectually. All his friends in high school were white. Clifford Apprey and Charles Gaston are interesting examples of how black identity may evolve in the lives of people who are affluent and integrated with whites at an early age. Charles Gaston was born and raised in a large northeastern city. Charles says that his high school was very segregated, and because he was in the honors program, his classes were "99 percent white." He took a nine-month European tour after graduation with four of his closest friends. When he returned, he met one of his father's friends who told him he was "the whitest black kid he had ever run across." The friend was a graduate of Brooks, and felt that Charles should consider attending Brooks for his college education. Charles told the friend, "It's not the real world. [It is a] second-rate education. You can't beat the Ivy League." After the friend offered him money if he applied, he accepted the offer, even though he had never heard of Brooks. After a semester he loved it—though he experienced "complete culture shock" when he arrived. Charles does not believe that there is a common experience that links all blacks, yet he feels he has more in common with blacks than with whites. When pressed on this issue, he relates the story of the rally he and Clifford attended for a local Republican candidate: ". . .within five minutes of everyone getting there all the black people were like this" (clasps hands to indicate togetherness).

Clifford and Charles both stated that there was no such thing as a "black identity." This seemed to contradict their earlier statements, so I probed further:

If there is no such thing as a black identity, why do we enter a room and go immediately to all the black people?

Clifford: When I walk into a room—I mean in a classroom the first black person I see I'm sitting right down and say "hey, buddy, we got three years—let's make it together."

Charles: I have a different answer for that. When I walk into a room, I know I have nothing in common with those people [whites]. More than likely I'll have something in common with at least one [black] person there—and even if I don't, it's a lot easier for me to be in a group and disagree with him [pointing to Clifford] than it is to disagree with them [whites].

Both of you have backgrounds in which you had early integration with whites, so it's interesting to me that you would say that you can walk into a room and feel that you don't have anything in common—

Charles: You know why? I'll give you a perfect example. When I came down here as a freshman my friend Jack Blumberg [a fictitious name] from high school—he went to Woodson. He pledged a fraternity. Called me up here at Brooks and he said "We're having a huge keg party. Why don't you come?" I said I have this friend—and he said, "Bring him." We went to Woodson. . . . We're dressed like everybody else. We have buttoned-down shirts, jeans, and loafers. When we got to the frat house everybody parted, looking at us like we were nuts. When I got to the door and knocked on the door I was like, "Is Jack Blumberg here?" Guy goes "hold on." Slams the door, runs inside, comes back out with Jack. . . . The guy who answered the door asked Jack "Are you in trouble? There's these two black guys outside asking for you." As if we're after him for something. . . . See, Jack failed to tell them we were black. He basically told them how we grew up together and they assumed I was white. From that point on though, we got less and less invitations to come to parties, or to hang out with him. And when we went home for Christmas break, I went to party [with the] same group of people I used to hang out with. And [I] noticed—I just don't have as much in common with these folks as I always thought.

Clifford echoes these sentiments and says that he has had the same experiences with white friends he had in boarding school. Charles does not communicate with or see any of the friends with whom he took the European vacation. It seems clear that after attending a black institution, Clifford and Charles's awareness of difference increased, which supports Demo and Hughes's (1990) assertion than diminished interracial contact increases feelings of black separatism.

Both Clifford and Charles have had experiences with racial discrimination. The experience that stands out in Clifford's mind happened in the fourth grade:

It was a majority-white class, and [the teacher] just had it out for me and my Spanish friend, Hosea. She made things very difficult. As a matter of fact, she told my father that she honestly felt that black kids didn't belong in gifted classes. And she went so far as to say that she was shocked that I tested for the gifted class. We had beat up desks. Everyone else had nice ones.

Charles remembers an incident when he participated in a summer program at an Ivy League university:

That was the first time I had ever experienced it [racism] head on. A white kid telling me that "Yea, you're stupid." All of my white friends from high school that were there sort of came to my rescue—"What are you talking about? You don't know him." That was the first time I had ever confronted somebody who said to my face "you're dumb."

Charles also recalls having dinner at the home of a young woman he was dating in high school and her uncles sitting at the dinner table conversationally using the word "nigger." He was shocked and did not know how to respond: "The thing is though that this one particular uncle turns to me and stuff and says, as if he was complimenting me, 'Angela tells me you're a smart nigger. I don't ever want to see you . . .

picking up them drugs. Cause you one of them smart niggers.'" Charles says that if that happened to him now, he would leave and never return.

At Brooks, their academic and social lives revolve around African-American culture; however, their political lives require close contact and interaction with the mostly white members of the Republican Party. They both perceive that the Republican Party is not prepared to deal with African-American members. Charles relates what happens when they attend Republican meetings or rallies in the state:

> Same thing you run into every day when you're around white people. It didn't matter that we had some of the same political ideology. We were still seen as—we were an anomaly. Oh, wow. People would come up to us, want to touch, want to talk to you. And it was very . . . it was you know . . . Jack Kemp, at one of the rallies had gotten up and we were laughing. We were like "he must want to run for President." He said, you know, "In order for us, the party is changing—a new Republican Party for everyone." Even we hollered "that's B.S."

Charles and Clifford balk at the notion of a black identity because they believe that such beliefs ostracize blacks who do not fit the mold—and these blacks may also have something to offer the larger community. However, if one eliminates the kinds of superficial cultural characteristics that many blacks have in common, these two young men do identify strongly with blacks. They believe that blacks should be responsible for helping less fortunate blacks. As Clifford Apprey pointed out, their conservatism is in the tradition of Du Bois, Washington, and Malcolm X. They are not the Newt Gingrich or Reagan-Bush kind of conservative. This is evident when their political attitudes are revealed in a series of questions about policies that may directly affect African-Americans.

The two men of Brooks College are certain about what conservative means to them—and that is that African-Americans are responsible for their own futures. This is Clifford's definition of what it means to be conservative:

> I think a lot of times when people hear that African-Americans are conservative Republicans they automatically think the worst—Jesse

Helms. That's not to say that every time, every time when I hear the word Democrat I think of John F. Kennedy or FDR. So, a lot of times there's no fair play around here. . . . Clarence Thomas, Thomas Sowell, Armstrong Williams, of course they're conservative but they don't represent others. To me Nat Turner was a conservative. W. E. B. Du Bois. I always argue with my friends that you can't name one African-American leader who was a liberal. . . . I think there are two types of conservatism. I think that when you talk about mainstream conservatism I don't think you're talking about anyone in this room. Americans' views of conservatives is anyone who is trying to save them money. I get the feeling when you say "I am a conservative" black people say "Oh, anti-affirmative action, oh, you sleep with Clarence Thomas." But what's funny is a lot of times—I had the hardest trouble coming to accept that I was conservative. Because there's such a stigma once you label yourself that. It's like "you're gay. No, I'm not gay, I just like to sleep with men." Those are the main thoughts . . . I really think that being conservative, honestly, is actually taking responsibility for the things we can control. Substance abuse, alcohol, all those things are tearing our community apart.

Clifford believes that African-Americans cannot afford to exclude any part of the community with rigid ideas about what it means to be black. The following are his ideas about how the black community could start to gain control of some of these problems:

Illegitimacy, we can start by counseling our own peers. Black on black violence—if every black church adopted a child, there wouldn't be a child here who couldn't pay for school. As a black conservative I say that the responsibility for our future lies within our own communities. I think the black church has a role to play in it. I think the mosque . . . I think Louis Farrakhan has just as much of a role as Calvin Butts does at Abyssinian Baptist Church in New York. Clarence Thomas has just as much of a role to play. Any African-American male, quite honestly, who is not in jail, is a voice. I don't care if you're gay or you're straight, any African-American male who is surviving on a day-to-day basis in America should be a part of our army. I think that too many times African-Americans like Jesse Jackson try and close ranks. "Well, Clarence Thomas is not with us." Well, what does it take to be black? Oh, is there a list we have? Black, OK, at one time you had to have kente cloth. See, I'm out. I mean, I guess I lose. There are blacks that will accuse blacks of not going to black schools—"You go to Yale? Man, you ain't black!"

Clifford is still struggling with the idea that his color has meaning in the United States. When he visits the country of his parents, he identifies with a tribal group. He says when he is in the United States, "it was like 'united we stand—divided we fall.' If you have that hue in your skin, no matter what the situation is, you have to stand with me. Even if I'm wrong, even if we're both wrong, we have to be there, no matter what." He is uncomfortable with Afrocentric philosophy, and finds it an unrealistic and romantic view of African culture.

Clifford and Charles believe that the emphasis on government remedies for black problems is misguided. This is one of the main reasons they find the Republican Party attractive. It is the party of independence from government solutions to social problems. Clifford reveals how he feels about the rhetoric of oppression:

> I always say African-Americans remind me of two persons who got dropped off in the forest, and instead of trying to get out, they sit there. "Can you believe we're stuck in the forest?" I say, "Well, let's go. Let's get out." "Can you believe someone dropped us off here? Oh, my God. Let's just sit here and hope someone comes back." And I think that ultimately that's what we do in a lot of cases. We wait [for] white America, after they've done all these things to us, to come back and say "we're going to fix it." We can't do that. We really can't.

Charles responds along similar lines. To him, conservatism means personal responsibility and responsibility for one's own community:

> Conservative. Responsible for your own successes and failures. No matter what example we may use . . . we may use business, our daily lives, the social situation of African-Americans. There's not a single situation we're in, positive or negative, that we didn't get into ourselves. It might have been help from some outside force, but that doesn't mean that we were coerced into it. Yes, I understand that cocaine comes from Columbia, and the U.S. government has to have a hand letting these people fly over our borders, 'cause you can't fly a prop plane over the ocean without getting caught. And, they may bring

them [drugs] into the ghetto, but we don't have to take them, you know? The Korean gentleman up on the corner might have a liquor store, but put him out of business. Don't buy his stuff.

The term moderate means "a person who doesn't take a hard line on every issue," according to Charles. Clifford does not believe in moderates. As for liberals, Charles said there were no true liberals, because "to me a true liberal is someone who is an unselfish person—who just is giving, giving, giving, without car[ing] basically for themselves. If someone were to tell me that President Clinton, or any Democrat up there in Washington were a true liberal, I would have to disagree with them." According to Clifford, a liberal is "anyone who loves me more than I love myself."

Charles and Clifford are clearly conservative because they support a philosophy of self-help. However, they are not individualists. They are community activists. They both support the welfare system. They both feel that fraud and abuse within the system should be stopped; however, they both agree that the system is for children. Clifford says,

> The average welfare mother is 25. She has two kids. She's only been on welfare for . . . 60 percent of the people on welfare leave within two years. I think welfare is about children. I think that's who welfare should really be for.

Charles adds, " . . . [children] should not be punished for the sins of the father [or] the shortcomings of the mother."

While they have a more liberal stance on welfare, both young men are less than enthusiastic about affirmative action. They resent the idea that affirmative action is perceived as a way of giving blacks an opportunity rather than allowing blacks to earn opportunities. Clifford is far less vocal than Charles on the subject. Charles spoke of the application process for colleges and conversations he had with his white classmates:

> I remember this guy, one of the most arrogant kids I've ever met in my life, got this huge debate in the cafeteria going about how Charles and Susan, another young lady, were going to get in the schools everyone was applying to because they're black. Never mind the fact that myself

and Susan were in the top 5 percent and top 12 percent of the class. Never mind the fact that we were doing much better than any of you; that we got higher SAT scores than any of you; higher AP scores than any of you . . . we're going to get in because we're black. So that prompted me to apply to every one of my schools and not fill in the race part of it. . . . It was the best day of my life when those acceptance letters started coming in.

Throughout the interview, Clifford Apprey made references to black leaders of the past. The only contemporary politician that they referred to positively was Jack Kemp. Since many black leaders have been compromised by scandal in recent years, these young conservatives were asked to talk about persons that they felt were good leaders for the black community. Both believe that Louis Farrakhan is an effective, persuasive, and powerful leader. Clifford Apprey contends that if Farrakhan were a Republican, he could win elective office. He believes that Farrakhan's weakest point is that he is a Muslim in a Christian country. When asked if Clifford believed Farrakhan to be an anti-Semite, he responded:

That's too strong a word.

How can you be a conservative Republican and be a fan of Louis Farrakhan? Do you not see any conflict there?

I don't see any conflict because my conservatism, my Republicanism, is for black people.

Brooks College is an unlikely place to find a young Republican Party organization. Charles and Clifford were asked how they survive on a campus where the political attitudes of most of the students are very different from their own. Most of the students can embrace the nationalist aspect of conservatism, but the Republican Party is a definite turnoff. It has been hard for Clifford and Charles to find an adviser for the Young Republicans and secure a meeting room. Recruiting new members is nearly impossible. Charles and Clifford are the only members of the organization who agreed to be interviewed. They say other members are "in the closet." They believe that more students agree with them than will admit it in class.

Clifford talks about a class he is taking:

I'm in a class called Racism and the Law. And it's like I am the Anti-Christ. We got into a thing about midnight basketball. Midnight basketball to me is the most racist thing. White America says, "Well, you know, we can't control y'all so for two hours we're going to make my Lexus safe. And my neighbor's Lexus safe. We're going to put you in the gym, and let you run up and down, and hopefully, you will be so tired, you'll go home and go to sleep." And that's it. Folks, if Republicans said the solution to the crime problem is let the kids play basketball, we would be in an uproar talking about "They're making us play sports again? This is racist!" The Democrats said this is a solution to a major problem. I say why don't they have midnight high school? Why not take that money and give kids jobs? Of course, African-Americans—we're in a dire situation. But that's ridiculous. That's racist social programming.

When asked why they might be so different from the other students at Brooks, Charles and Clifford point out that they have been strongly influenced by their fathers. Charles's father owns several businesses and works for a large company. His mother is a homemaker. Charles says of his father, "I have a father at home who has basically shown me everything I need to know. Anytime we speak [nodding at Clifford], I quote my Dad. Even people who have their Dads at home, a lot of times [they] are not as involved." Charles's father is a conservative and a Republican. He considers his mother "apolitical." He and his father discuss politics often, and Charles derives most of his views from conversations with his father and by observing the way his father works.

Clifford says he was "flabbergasted" when he found that many of his college classmates had never met their fathers. He and Charles talk so much about their fathers, Clifford describes it as bordering on "hero worship." He believes that he and Charles have alienated some of their classmates because he and Charles speak so highly of their fathers. Clifford calls his father "a bleeding-heart liberal." His father worked hard to provide the best education for his children, and, Clifford says, "He never accepted help or made excuses." In spite of his father's liberal political attitudes, Clifford says that his views were influences by his father's actions, not by his words.

The statement about the strength of their fathers as breadwinners and role models speaks to the value placed on economic independence and control in the lives of these young men. Perceived control over one's destiny is a critical component of self-esteem among young black men (Tashakkori 1993). The Republican Party is attractive because it supports the idea that individuals are in control, and systemic inequities may be overcome. Charles and Clifford have modified this idea somewhat by transforming individual responsibility to community responsibility, specifically, the *black* community's responsibility. This theme of community responsibility for improving the lives of blacks as a group is repeated among students who share Clifford and Charles's partisan identity, but lean more toward the ideas of Booker T. Washington than Louis Farrakhan.

The "Old School" Conservatives—Young Black Republicans

Chris Gray—Barnett University

These young conservatives differ from the young men at Brooks in significant ways. They are more rigid on moral and cultural issues as well as welfare. They also believe that there is a black identity, and that blacks differ in significant ways from whites. One student, Chris Gray, wants to return to the days when, because of segregation, blacks lived and conducted business within their own communities. He believes this environment was a healthier one for blacks since it encouraged the development of businesses and fostered a sense of unity.

Chris is one of the leaders of the Republican Party organization on campus. He is from the Southeast—and was raised in an upper-middle-class black neighborhood. Chris's parents are both professionals. His mother is active in liberal causes, and he considers his father a "conservative Democrat," as he was until he became disillusioned with Democratic Party ideas on welfare and other social programs. The private military academy Chris attended in high school, along with his father's influence, molded his conservative ideas. Working for George Bush in the 1988 and 1992 campaigns "changed his mind"—in a conservative direction—about some issues, and he is now active in statewide Republican politics.

Chris says that he does not think about his identity as a black person much, because he is always around black people at the university. He believes that there is a black identity, though it comes from "knowing who you are and where you're from. Koreans, Jewish, and Italians all have that in them. They know who they are and where they come from. I think that black people do have that." He also thinks that black identity takes many forms:

> The black identity is so diverse. I don't like it when people say you're acting black. I guess acting ghetto is supposed to be acting black. Sometimes they say that. But you can be black and come in a three-piece suit, you can talk with a so-called white . . . you can talk that way . . . you're still black.

Chris feels that some black conservatives do not have a black identity, because in part "it's a mind-set that sets you apart from anyone else." When asked what that mind-set is, he explains that it is related to one's willingness to help blacks who are less fortunate. According to Chris, "Black people are very generous people. I think your going back to help out those behind you is a major characteristic." For Chris, black identity is, at core, the obligation one feels to help those blacks who need help—not on superficial criteria such as language or mannerisms.

Chris defines conservative as maintaining the status quo. He does not believe moderates exist; however, liberals want to change everything and expand social programs. One of the issues about which Chris feels strongly is gay rights. He does not approve of Clinton's "Don't Ask, Don't Tell" policy, and would like to see gay men and women banned from the military. Chris says that "the military is a hostile environment. It's different from the teaching profession or any other profession. The military is dealing with lives that can be taken or can be had at any time." He is not sure how this explains why gays should be banned from the military, but is convinced that it has something to do with trust.

He also says he does not like affirmative action, although he thinks there is still a need for such programs:

> I think there's a need for it right now because blacks need to catch up to white people. I think if this were a perfect society we wouldn't need it—but it's not, and blacks are at a disadvantage right now. I think that Clarence Thomas and J. C. Watts and the rest of the Republicans are wrong to try to get rid of affirmative action because they would not be in the position they're in right now if it weren't for affirmative action.

However, when Chris is asked to agree or disagree with a statement asking whether minorities should be given special consideration in hiring, he disagrees. He also agrees with the statement that job applicants should be judged solely on the basis of test scores and other individual qualities.

He believes the government should help blacks by ensuring racial equality, but he is not sure how that would be done. Chris says that the problems in the black community are perpetuated and heightened by the media. The media affects the self-image of young blacks by reflecting only negative images:

> The main thing they show is us getting shot and getting arrested. . . . [They] don't show the positive that we do in the community every day. If you do something positive, it has to be on a grand, grand scale. They don't really [show] the individuals who are packing lunches for charities. They don't show that. If you watch the news you think that the only thing we do is get arrested and go to homeless shelters and the white people come down to the shelters at Christmas and Easter and they give black people food. And that's how we live.

Chris blames the media for black problems but says the problems can best be solved by the family. Parents should take responsibility for their children, and "the black church needs to come back." Chris would like to see the rebuilding of black communities so that they return to the community he knew as a child: "When I was younger, our neighbors used to get me if I did something wrong. I don't really see that happening any more." Chris also blames problems in the community on a lack of black leadership. He feels that black organizations such as the NAACP and the Urban League are faltering and ineffective.

When asked to finish the statement "If blacks don't do well in life it is because," Chris replies that lack of opportunity is the main reason:

Black people weren't given the opportunities that white people were given, or that other minorities were given. That's one of the reasons they don't succeed. Also, some black people don't . . . they use it as a crutch, as an excuse. I've seen that a lot of times. Oh, the white man didn't give me. I think if you get something—if you get an opportunity—you need to take advantage of it. Even if you don't, I think you need to work as hard as you can to obtain what you can, even if it's not that Ferrari or that Lexus. Do what you can do.

Chris Gray is more conservative on the subjects of welfare, abortion, and gay rights than his counterparts at Brooks. However, he shares with them the belief that blacks can do more to help themselves. He also shares with them the presence of an influential father. Chris does not say that his father shaped his views; however, his father is characterized as a conservative Democrat. His mother, he says, is a true liberal. Chris has become a Republican, but he and his father are closer in ideology than he and his mother. Chris admires Louis Farrakhan, and believes that if he were a part of mainstream politics, he would be a Republican. When asked about Farrakhan's separatist views, Chris replies that Farrakhan is expressing sentiments that mirror those of white conservatives. Chris is not a separatist, but he does feel that integration has caused black businesses to suffer. He also thinks that the exodus of middle-class blacks from black neighborhoods in cities has been a major factor in the decline of the black community. Chris Gray, Clifford Apprey, and Charles Gaston are disappointed in the quality of leadership from established African-American organizations. They see Louis Farrakhan as the most capable and effective leader for the black community.

Cornell Hall—Barnett University

One of Chris's fellow Republican Party members at Barnett is Cornell Hall, a bright and animated young man raised in the Northeast in predominantly white upper-class communities. Both parents are professionals, but Cornell makes it clear that his father is the person with whom he discusses politics, and who has the greatest influence on his life.

Cornell has experienced several identity crises, and believes that much of his difficulty stemmed from being part of such a small minority in his community and school. He says that whites resented his family's presence in the community. His last name, not revealed here, has a decidedly aristocratic ring. He was often teased about having such a name. He describes his identity crises as having several phases, and says he did not realize what being black meant until he was in the seventh grade. When he was in the seventh grade, all his friends were white.

The behavior of the black students that were bused in from the working-class neighborhoods encouraged his "antiblack" phase. Cornell did not like these students to call attention to themselves with bad behavior. He says that he would think to himself, "They're making me—they're not representing—they're not doing it right!" When asked why he thought the students had to represent anything, he replies that he felt that if all the blacks behaved as a team, performing well in class and not getting into any trouble, it would "take away the ridicule." Cornell was embarrassed if a black person came to speak at his middle school and did not speak standard English: "I'd cringe. Why would I cringe? Because I knew they [the other students] would talk about him."

His "antiblack" phase in seventh grade was followed by his "black militant" phase. This "black militant" phase was probably due to Cornell's "encounter" experience. He and his mother were shopping in an exclusive department store, and his mother was being treated in a condescending manner by a store clerk. Cornell was "furious," and knew for the first time deep within himself that his mother was being treated that way because she was black. This phase lasted from the eighth grade until his junior year in high school. When asked what being "really black" meant to him during this phase, Cornell replied:

> Well, you see I know that being black is not what you wear. And I knew it then and know it's not any of that. But, that's how people thought. That's how the kids acted. They acted like they believed that so I just went along with it. So I was making friends. These were students who lived right by the tracks so they would try to be cool or whatever. Before I would be wearing khaki pants and loafers. Then I started wear-

ing Georgetown shirts and hats. I started wearing tennis shoes more. Just whatever I saw my friends wearing—my new friends.

Finally there was his "settling" phase, which lasted until he graduated from high school. He remains friends with the blacks who became his friends in the eighth grade, but has no contact with his white friends. Cornell says that "Right now I'm more 'white,' or who I was before all this mess." What Cornell means is that if people perceive that being "white" means wearing khaki trousers and buttoned-down Oxford shirts, which is his current outfit, then he is being "white." He laughs and says that at Barnett he is "free" to be himself.

Black identity for Cornell is about the sharing of oppression. When asked what a young man with his life chances might have in common with a young man living in Cabrini Green housing project in Chicago, Cornell said:

> We share the system. We share America. And the way America deals with us and the way white America treats us. It is the commonality of suffering, it is a commonality of abuse, it is a commonality, you know, I can't drive down the street—and we all share this. And I don't know why people like Clarence Thomas are so ignorant to deny it occurs. I'm sure he encounters this. I don't know why he lies to himself. We all share racism and the legacy of slavery.

Cornell believes that black culture differs from white culture in "the way we raise our kids." He says that black parents are stricter disciplinarians because they have different cultural mores. He cites his observations of white friends whose parents were more tolerant than his parents of risky behaviors such as reckless driving.

When Cornell was in high school, he perceived that white teachers felt that he did not deserve to be a student in that school. He was frustrated by the inability of other black students to understand what was happening to them:

> What upset me the most is, you know, when black students didn't recognize what was happening. 'Cause then they were really being victimized. They don't know what's going on, and so, you know, I guess . . . I saw a lot of kids who I thought were really bright who were in lower classes. And they had no business being there—especially black males.

Cornell believes that black parents need to be especially conscientious when their children are in majority-white schools to prevent all black students from ending up in lower level classes. He says that in this environment he felt that he could never afford to make a mistake.

By the time Cornell was a high school junior or senior, he decided that he would become completely silent in class. This was a deliberate strategy to eliminate the conflict he was having with white teachers. This silence was accompanied by superlative performance on assignments and exams, and was meant as a sort of rebellion against the injustices suffered by other black students. Cornell feels that excellence and integrity are essential elements in the lives of blacks. He calls this being "above reproach," and explains his nonparticipation in class this way:

> . . . I would go to class and fold my hands and wouldn't say a word. The teachers would be mad because I wasn't saying anything. And they'd just nitpick and look for any old thing—but I was ABOVE RE-PROACH. [Cornell emphasizes these words with volume and clear enunciation.] I'm saying, you know, that for the first two years I was going through all this stuff. In the last two years I realized that we really need to be better. We need to, you know, be more careful about what we do and what we say and who we're around. And I just started becoming "above reproach." And I continue that legacy until this day.

The Clarence Thomas/Anita Hill debacle convinced Cornell that his philosophy of being "above reproach" was a good one. He thinks that black leaders, and black people in general, cannot afford to behave in ways that could lead to the kinds of accusations faced by Clarence Thomas.

When asked what being a conservative means, Cornell identifies an issue that is the dividing line between conservatives and liberals: abortion. He is pro-life, and believes this issue may be the one that will seriously divide the country. As a member of the Republican Party, Cornell also feels the need to defend the notion that Republicans are racist:

> White people are racists. That's just a fact. I'm not saying all of them are, but a lot of them are regardless of their political affiliation. OK,

Democrats are more open-minded and liberal than Republicans. Then, all right, OK, you step back and take a look at the issues. OK. What's important to you? What do you think is going to help our people? What do you think—you know, a lot of people think that oh, if you're a Republican, you're a sellout, you're a this, you're a that. Now, let's think about this for a second. If there's no one who is a Republican, right, why should they ever care about a bunch of black people? You know, they would never do anything unless there are some people who are watching them. Just like there are white people in the NAACP, white people here at Barnett, watching us, seeing what we're doing. There are black people watching Republicans, and seeing what they're doing.

Cornell laughingly says separatism is not the answer because a black state would be "too easy to pick off." He also believes that it is not healthy for all blacks to be Democrats, nor is it healthy for all blacks to be conservative Republicans. Moderates, in Cornell's view, try to be "politically correct." They are more like conservative Democrats. Liberals, he says, are "fringe groups." Fringe groups include radical feminists, pro-choice groups, and gay rights groups. Cornell would not like any harm to come to members of the gay community, but says he is "*so offended* by comparisons of the movement for gay rights with the movement for black rights." He believes that being gay is a choice, which distinguishes it from being black.

Cornell's conservative views on abortion and gay rights do not extend to affirmative action. He believes affirmative action remains a viable program because corporations continue to discriminate against black men. He believes the government can play a role in helping to ensure racial equality by encouraging the retention of affirmative action.

Cornell is not sure how welfare should be reformed, but believes that "welfare is a crutch to us." Cornell thinks that the availability of welfare payments does not help to develop individuals—it is an allowance that encourages subservience. He opposes premarital sex and those who think that the distribution of condoms is a good way to prevent pregnancy and disease. For Cornell, this is just another example of the popular belief that blacks have no control over themselves. Abstaining from sex and drugs is, for Cornell, simply a matter of self-control.

All the African-American leaders Cornell admires are from traditional politics. He is enamored of Andrew Young and Thurgood Marshall, and respects Louis Farrakhan; however, he disapproves of the latter's rhetoric. Cornell is comfortable with himself, dressed in his khakis and buttoned-down shirt—and he identifies with blacks while placing the responsibility for improving conditions in the community squarely on the shoulders of blacks. When asked to complete the sentence "If blacks don't do well in life it is because," Cornell replied that "he or she didn't take the initiative to move on. The system is weighted against us. But I do not believe that because things are hard, we can't make it. It should be an incentive for us."

Summary

The conservative views of these students present a serious ideological paradox. On the one hand, these young men have pledged themselves to a political party that repels most African-Americans. On the other hand, they purport to work for black interests. They defend their membership in the Republican Party by saying that Democrats condescend to blacks and have crippled them economically. This defense may have merit, but it is not satisfactory. They admit to feeling less than welcome at Republican Party functions, yet they remain members.

One explanation for this paradox is simple. These students have no political home for their ideas. The Democrats promote a liberal agenda that they find objectionable. The Nation of Islam requires converting to a religion and a Spartan lifestyle. Additionally, leader Louis Farrakhan's rhetoric may be too extreme to permit a full embrace of his philosophy. This leaves them with the option of joining the Republican Party and attempting to carve out a niche for themselves.

A second explanation for this paradox is more complicated. As products of dual-parent, upper-middle-class homes, these young men are frustrated by their inability to distinguish themselves from blacks who are from impoverished environments. As they have grown into young adulthood, their experiences have heightened this frustration. They are keenly aware that a good deal of racial prejudice is based on the assumption that all blacks are "ghetto" blacks. They resent this assumption, which is evidenced by Clifford and Charles's admonitions against defining an "authentic" black identity. Chris and Cornell also state clearly that being black does not include speaking or dressing in any way that is different from white Americans.

This race-class dilemma is perhaps exacerbated by the expectation that men are supposed to make it on their own—"fight the good fight" and so forth. Charles's story of not marking the race category on his college applications because of accusations of special privilege revealed the potency of this expectation. The notion that blacks need help and government programs to solve their problems is an affront to their class and gender identities. To reconcile this multiple-group identity, (being black, male, and middle class), they adopt a conservative ideology to establish their independence from the black masses. They then justify this ideology by connecting it to strategies for rebuilding the black community. Clifford Apprey of Brooks College pointed out that the great black leaders of the past were conservative. Making this connection also allows them to establish their independence from the white-male dominated Republican Party.

Clifford Apprey and Charles Gaston value the idea of a single political vision or purpose to be fulfilled by the black community, while eschewing ideas of a "black identity." Their political goal is to improve the lives of black Americans and solve the problems of crime, poverty, and ignorance. A unity of purpose, in their view, should take precedence over ideological differences within the black community.

The "old school" conservatives believe that there is a black identity. For Chris, this identity has to do with the obligation one feels to help poorer blacks. For Cornell, this identity is the shared experience of oppression. Cornell was not as enthusiastic as Chris, Clifford, and Charles regarding the leadership of Louis Farrakhan. Chris and Cornell also put more emphasis on individual responsibility for economic conditions than do Clifford and Charles.

These young men, while citing some experiences with racial discrimination, do not acknowledge that these experiences had any profound effect on them. Chris Gray claims never to have experienced racial discrimination. Chris mentioned that he believed his mother experienced racial discrimination while growing up because she was "down South," but because she had never spoken of her experiences, he was not sure. The parents of the Republican race men have uniformly neglected to talk about their experiences with racism with their children. This is not an uncommon phenomenon. In his book *Mississippi*, Anthony Walton writes about his discovery of the horrors his father experienced growing up in the South. Walton was bewildered by the racial hatred expressed by white residents of Bensonhurst, New York, in the 1989 protest march against the death of Yusef Hawkins.[2] He decided to return to the South to explore the source of racial hatred. It was during this odyssey that the truth of his father's experiences were revealed.

Socioeconomic status may have shielded these young people from encounters with overt racism. However, it must be noted that they seemed reluctant to attribute some of their experiences to race. A possible explanation for this is that they were sensitive to the notion that blacks are "whiners," and did not want to be categorized as such.

While these young men voted for Bush in the 1992 presidential election, approximately 80 percent of blacks voted for Clinton in 1992. In the 1988 Bush/Dukakis race, 25 percent of black Republicans cast their vote for Dukakis. In 1992, 29 percent of black Republicans cast their vote for Bill Clinton (Bolce, DeMaio, and Muzzio 1993). The Republican message of small government and individual responsibility is not penetrating the black community as a whole. The stability of the marriage between Republican Party politics and black activism revealed by these students will be tested as members of the post–civil rights generation come to political maturity.

3

The Conservatives, Part 2

The Traditional Conservatism of the South and the Struggle against Black Stereotypes

The Republican "race men" of the previous chapter are conservative and possess a strong racial group identity. As Clifford Apprey said, his conservatism and his Republicanism are "for black people." The students in this chapter are also conservative, but their conservatism was not born of a desire for new solutions to black problems. They are not followers or supporters of Louis Farrakhan, and they do not feel that blacks necessarily have an obligation to help other blacks. Their conservatism is the result of their being born and raised in the conservative South, their religiosity, and their need to counter images of black irresponsibility and dependence. For two of the students in this chapter, upper-middle-class socioeconomic status, conservative parents, and a rejection of African-American commonality are at the root of their conservative ideology.

Southerners are more conservative, and more religious, than people in other regions of the country, with rural southerners being more conservative than urban southerners. For example, while black support for busing has wavered in all regions of the country, southerners are more opposed to it than northerners (Schuman, Steeh, and Bobo 1985). Another illustration of such regional differences (rural and urban) among blacks is found in the historical development of the Nation of Islam. The Nation, with its fiery call for a separate black nation, never resonated with black southerners (Jaynes and Williams 1989). It was the northern urban black who suffered most from economic downturns, crime, and drug addiction. Founded in the 1930s by Elijah Muhammed, the Nation of Islam established fifty mosques by 1959, only seven of which were located in the South.

Blacks in the South tend not to embrace black nationalist ideology, but to identify with an assimilationist ideology instead. These assimilationist sentiments may be a legacy from the civil rights movement. Separatism may also be perceived as a cousin of segregation—a symbol of inferiority. Support for integration combined with southern religiosity is only part of the reason these students are more inclined to embrace a conservative ideology. The other part of the story may have to do with parental influence, enervated black political leadership, and a growing conservative religious movement.

We know that religiosity may encourage civil organization and participation (Calhoun-Brown 1996; Harris 1994; Smith and Seltzer 1992). We also know that religiosity has not—at least not so far—been linked with conservatism on welfare or other economic issues. This may be changing with the post–civil rights generation. The students in this chapter give credence to the notion that religiosity encourages civic participation—they are active in political, fraternal, and service organizations as well as their churches. They are also fairly conservative on moral and cultural issues, as we would expect (Tate 1994). However, they are also somewhat conservative on welfare, and are not convinced that poor blacks are helped by this kind of government assistance.

One explanation for their conservatism on welfare is the conservative philosophy that underpins many of the ministries in the black evangelical movement, which is gaining influence within the black community. Prominent leaders in this movement, such as T. D. Jakes of Dallas, Texas, have endorsed the predominantly white and conservative Promise Keepers, a religious organization dedicated to inspiring men to develop "Christlike masculinity" by becoming better husbands, fathers, and citizens (Biblical Discernment Ministries 1997). Jakes also sponsors conferences called "Manpower," that are similar to Promise Keepers, where he advises men that meeting their family's financial needs is part of living a disciplined Christian life (Walker 1996). A. R. Bernard, a prominent Church of God in Christ (COGIC) minister in New York City, preaches "discipline, self-reliance, and financial independence" to his mostly male congregation (Toler 1996). These developments are important in that the messages of financial independence and traditional roles for men and women are layered over messages of sexual abstinence and marital fidelity. It is easy to see the connection between these ideas and nonsupport for welfare. While the students in this chapter did not specifically refer to any of the above ministries during the interviews, this may be an area that warrants further exploration.

The students interviewed in this chapter recognize racial group membership as important, but are less likely than their urban counterparts to view it as an overriding factor in their lives. Two of the students, Curtis Foster, and Corliss Bond, are from two-parent, working-class families in rural communities. Conrad Terry is from a two-parent working- to middle-class household in a midsized city. The other two students, Carol Changa and Carl Franks, are from two-parent, upper-class households, and grew up in larger cities.

Southern Comforts: Convention and Christianity

Curtis Foster—Benedict University

Curtis Foster is from a small town in the South, and works while he attends graduate school at Benedict. He has not traveled more than a few hundred miles from home, and seems content with the quality of life in the region. Raised in an all-black neighborhood, Curtis's parents were hardworking people who found time to be involved in their children's lives. His mother, who held clerical jobs, once took an entire summer's leave from her job to help him reach the appropriate grade level in reading. His father is a blue-collar worker who spent long hours away from home. Curtis characterizes his parents as "apolitical," and says that they voted, but never talked about politics or race relations in the home.

Curtis was a college student when he first traveled by plane. He identifies this experience as one which made him realize that he was different, and that this difference was related to his racial group membership. Prior to taking this trip he had only been around blacks, and was unaware that his racial group membership had any significance. Curtis and his friends felt free to do what they wanted. Although he had heard about racism, he had never been "pushed up against it." When he arrived at the airport, he had no conception of how to board the plane or how to check his luggage. Curtis explains why this experience made him aware of race:

> I was talking with this guy because I didn't know anything. I didn't know how to read the . . . I knew this was the plane ticket. It was a white guy and he said "Are you sure you should be here?" And I'm like, what are the questions, all I want to know is where to go to get on the plane. I saw that I wasn't being treated equally because the next person that came up he was saying "Hi, how are you? What can I do to help you?" It was just something that . . . I was a black male. He related to them [the next customer] a lot better than he did me. I really felt out there. I didn't feel comfortable any more. Then I looked around and most of the people were white. And I'm thinking, gosh, I must be black. Or gosh, I'm the only one out here. I felt by myself.

Curtis only thinks about what he has in common with other blacks "once in a while." He believes that what happens to other blacks in this country will affect him only somewhat—but being black is more important to him than being American. A black identity for Curtis is rooted in knowing the history of blacks in this country. He says, "Knowing where you came from, knowing your history, so when they [whites] come up with a famous doctor, you can, too. When they say 'President Clinton' you can say 'Jesse Jackson.'" Curtis feels that being able to tell whites about your history makes them more tolerant of differences, since "we know all about them and they know nothing about us."

Curtis has never experienced overt racial discrimination, and has never heard racial epithets used by whites. He does know of a friend who had a confrontation with a white man on a beach while trying out a new video camera. As he was panning over the beach area, he happened to tape a young white woman sunning herself on the beach. According to Curtis, this is what followed:

Her boyfriend—they couldn't distinguish whether it was her boyfriend or her Daddy—he was an older man, said, and just to show you how they do 'cause they do it all the time. Just the way that man said, he asked him, "Boy, what are you doing?" He said, "I'm just video-taping." He [the older white man] said, "you shouldn't be videotaping our women."

After asking the man to repeat the phrase, his friend refused to stop taping. It was then that the man became threatening and called his friend a "nigger," after which the friend left the beach. Curtis says this was the first time he had even heard of someone being called a "nigger" by a white person. Curtis Foster is now aware that blacks are vulnerable to mistreatment by others because of race, but he has been spared some of the harsher treatment experienced by some of the liberal students. This may have had an impact on his views, which are surprisingly conservative.

Conservatives, in Curtis's view, "go with the basics" and want to maintain the status quo, while moderates understand both sides of an issue. Liberals are "feisty" in that they push for change. They are also more inclusive; they can "deal with all colors." He considers both his parents to be conservative because although they vote, they have never been involved in civil rights or political movements of any sort. Curtis considers himself liberal; most likely because he has a few liberal attitudes regarding issues like affirmative action. However, as we shall see, Curtis is not as liberal as he believes himself to be.

Curtis's observations at his workplace have influenced his perspective on affirmative action. He was not certain about it before he began working. Now he believes it is necessary, mainly because blacks throughout his workplace are regularly passed over for promotions without explanation. People with less knowledge and experience than he have been promoted over him. He is "all for thinking that the best candidate should be the right person" for a position. Yet he believes that even when a minority is the right person for the job, he or she is unlikely to be selected because of cultural barriers:

You have to get out there and act like them. You almost have to change the way that you act as a black person to be like them so they will choose you. Although they choose you only because you have some of the same characteristics, and not because they really want you. It's because you fit that mold. You have to wear the same white shirt, you know, made by the same company so it'll look the same way. You have to talk like them. You have to laugh at the silly jokes that they have.

Even though Curtis thinks affirmative action is necessary, his ambivalence is evident when he gives a neutral response to the statement "job applicants should be judged solely on the basis of test scores and other individual qualities." He does not attribute the failure of individual blacks to discrimination, completing the statement "If black people don't do well in life it is because" with "of lack of self-esteem." For Curtis, the most pressing problem in the black community is a lack of income and awareness of the importance of education and political participation, which for him are connected. Curtis provides more evidence that he may not be the liberal he thinks he is when he leaves government out of his solution to this problem, preferring that successful blacks take on the problem by mentoring young blacks in troubled communities. He is currently working with such a project, and reveals an inclination toward an individualist philosophy when queried about his opinion on government spending.

Curtis would like to see increased spending on social programs such as midnight basketball. Unlike Clifford and Charles, two of the Republican race men, Curtis thinks that midnight basketball is a good idea. He does not, however, think that welfare spending should be increased, because "if you know that you have the support it might prevent you from putting forth much effort." The government spends "a little too much" on welfare. It "hinders people a little bit." Curtis approves of short-term government assistance for people in a crisis; however, he still believes that welfare recipients should work—if only as volunteers.

Curtis's conservative bent is more pronounced on moral and cultural issues. He opposes abortion under any circumstances, and disapproves of premarital sex and having children outside marriage. He is only fairly tolerant on homosexuality. When it comes to women's rights, he is supportive of equal treatment under the law, but balks at the notion of women forging careers. He believes that nurturing a career interferes with a woman's ability to fulfill her primary responsibility, which is the family. It is the woman's job to rear children "from birth up," because she does a much better job of it than men.

Curtis declares that his partisan identification is as an Independent, which is not surprising considering the mix of conservative and liberal views revealed in the interview. He voted for Clinton in 1992 because "I liked him. I liked his views about things—especially health." He also thought that Clinton brought a "sense of unity" to the country. Curtis admires Maxine Waters (D-CA), a black House member who represents part of South Central Los Angeles. Although Maxine Waters is not shy in her advocacy for black interests, Curtis's admiration does not extend to another vocal advocate of black interests, Louis Farrakhan. Curtis is confused by what he perceives as mixed messages in Farrakhan's rhetoric: "I can't understand how he says love everybody and then says hate all the white people." He concedes, however, that "it's strange," but Farrakhan is probably the most influential leader today.

Curtis Foster's nearly absent racial group identity has been awakened by his work experience. He has led a sheltered life, which is demonstrated by the fact that he grew up in an extremely segregated community and remained unaware of racial differences. Here again the lack of exposure and interaction with whites has resulted in a freedom from racial considerations. Only when Curtis entered a "white" world—for example, the airport near his small town—did it occur to him that being black had significance in his life. As he so aptly stated, he had never been "pushed up against" racism, so there was never any reason for him to think about the economic or social consequences of his racial group membership. Now that he is working, he has discovered that promotions do not come as easily to blacks as they do to whites. Affirmative action is now real for him, as is the significance of racial group membership.

Curtis's "encounter" stage in the development of his racial group identity has been gradual. The mild snubbing of the airport official was an unremarkable initiation. The frustration he experiences on the job is also mildly irritating to him, mainly because this is a short-term situation. After he receives his master's degree, he expects to move on to greener pastures. If Curtis has an experience that is more severely disappointing as a result of his race, he may become less conservative. Until then, his conservative viewpoints on solutions to black problems will remain intact.

His strong belief in the value of work, a significant characteristic of southern culture, is evident in his attitudes on welfare. This factor, combined with the fact that he considers himself "very religious" (he is an active member of a Baptist church with traditional tenets), may influence his attitudes on women having careers. Curtis's main concern regarding racial issues is affirmative action, which he believes in because of his perception that discrimination in his own workplace continues. What may be more important is the fact that Curtis does not look to government for solutions to problems of poverty, drugs, and crime in the black community, which explains his nonsupport of welfare and perhaps his ambivalence on affirmative action.

Southern Currents: Political Involvement and Collective Action

Conrad Terry—Benedict University

The tremendous increase in black elected officials over the past twenty years is the result of increased opportunities to run, and to win, in majority-black districts, as well as the burgeoning black middle class. The black middle class, possessing greater material and organizational resources, feels more politically efficacious than before. This has resulted in a significant amount of political participation (Shingles 1981). In the South, there are still compelling reasons to organize around the election of black officials. Although Curtis Foster is part of the "integration generation," most of his life has been spent in segregated environments. This is not as uncommon as one might think for his generation, especially in this region. This segregated environment encourages African-American political mobilization, and is one of the reasons why Curtis Foster identified political participation as a key element in rebuilding poor black communities. The next student is politically active on and off campus. Like Curtis Foster, he considers himself an Independent, and would like to see African-Americans take more responsibility for conditions in their communities.

Conrad Terry, who grew up in the largest city in his southern state, is grooming himself to head the student organization at Benedict. He is a scholar-athlete and has a close relative who is making a name for himself in local politics. Conrad supports the relative by working hard in his campaigns. He attended integrated elementary and middle schools, but his high school was predominantly black. Conrad's father runs several small businesses, and his mother has a pink-collar job with a large food company. Money was scarce while he was growing up, and Conrad remembers days when there was little to eat.

Unlike Curtis, Conrad remembers becoming aware of racial differences at a very early age—perhaps because he attended an integrated kindergarten, while Curtis was not integrated with whites until he began working. Conrad was in kindergarten where his best friend, a white girl, joined him in a reading group every day. When the teachers stopped her from doing this, he knew instinctively that it had something to do with his being black. Conrad was angry with his friend for allowing the teachers to stop her from being in the reading group. Now he laughs at his failure to understand that she had no choice in the matter.

Conrad thinks about being black a lot, and believes that what happens to other blacks will affect him a great deal. When asked if he could define a black identity, Conrad replied, "You can't be black and not have a black identity. Identifying, I believe, is initiated from one person onto another person. Others have a part in molding or shaping your identity." In other words, the perception others have of black people and the ways in which black people relate to other black people, means that no black can escape this identity. Conrad's response was significantly different from any other response to this question; it suggests that for Conrad others are just as responsible as blacks for making race an issue.

Conrad's experiences with racism help explain why he feels that others make it difficult to escape identifying with race. Once when there was an assault in the neighborhood surrounding his high school, Conrad and a friend were stopped by the police while leaving track practice, made to get out of the car, and place their hands in the air. The officers searched the car and refused to tell them why they had been stopped or why the car was being searched:

> I was really upset. What had happened was the person involved in the fight left in a Volkswagen bug. The bug was red. The bug we were sitting in was gray. The windows were tinted—they didn't see whether or not the guy was white, or black. I guess they just assumed—they were two white cops—they just assumed that the guy who beat this brother down was a black guy. We had on *track* shoes, the *whole nine*.

The second incident, a more violent one, happened when he was fifteen. He was called a "nigger" by a group of older white boys who lived in a trailer park near his neighborhood. He and his friend tried to ignore them, but a fight ensued. According to Conrad, "it turned into a really verbally abusive situation before it became a fight. He was calling my friend's mother a bitch and spat in his face. It was just ridiculous."

In spite of these experiences, however, Conrad is committed to traditional methods of achieving racial equality—through electoral politics and community effort. He defines political conservatism as merely "reserved"—made up of broad-minded people who simply prefer quiet solutions to social problems. Moderates are "kind of in between" and liberals are concerned with the collective good. Liberals want to reach out to everyone, and are more inclusive of minorities. He thinks his mother is "a definite liberal," while his father is conservative. He believes he is more conservative than liberal. Conrad has been influenced by the work of black leaders during the civil rights movement, but thinks more blacks need to be in the conservative camp, "because we need individuals—to me it's a title, OK? It doesn't mean you have to act accordingly." For Conrad, liberals sometimes approach issues more directly than he would like—they have an in-your-face method of dealing with race issues. He prefers a quieter way of doing things, and in that sense, he says, he is definitely conservative.

Conrad has been influenced in a liberal direction by the "Contract with America,"[1] which he believes divides Americans:

It fails to embrace those things that affect people as a whole. It is a movement that will not only weaken blacks and minorities, but will weaken the core of America by leaving out the important things— children's education, the education of young folk like myself, and welfare as well. I really feel that the bottom line to the U.S. [financial] situation is, I'll put it simply, "getting up off the money." When I say "getting up off the money" we're talking about minimum wage, making people interested in being employed.

In Conrad's view, the current minimum wage is inadequate. For him, this is proved by a study that revealed that most welfare-dependent single mothers worked at minimum-wage jobs. This is Conrad's pragmatic side—putting more money directly in people's pockets, he thinks, is bound to help change their condition.

Conrad characterizes most of his friends as conservative. He joins his friends in his nonsupport of affirmative action, although he does think government should "enforce rules and laws that prohibit racial inequalities." Conrad sees a lack of education and knowledge about financial matters as the source of problems in the black community. Those problems would best be solved by "educating ourselves and others about what it means to invest safely." He also believes blacks should make acquiring an education a "personal endeavor." Ultimately, black people are responsible for improving their own communities. When it is clear that present strategies are ineffective, new ones should be developed. This belief in self-help does not prevent Conrad from citing external reasons for the failure of individual blacks. He finishes the statement, "In the United States, if black people don't do well in life, it is because" with "they didn't have the proper nourishment, as well as the proper tools for succeeding. Those tools are a proper education as well as a support system."

Conrad thinks welfare spending is "about right" and more funds should be allocated for criminal rehabilitation. He is pro-choice, tolerant of premarital sex, intolerant of out-of-wedlock births, and neutral on homosexuality. Conrad voted for Clinton in 1992 because "he made blacks feel that there was a chance for something good to happen with him." Education is important to Conrad, but it is a "personal" endeavor. He makes no mention of government assistance or the development of programs to help people obtain an education. The only government intervention he supports is an increase in the minimum wage, because it may serve as an incentive to welfare recipients. It is also worth noting that Conrad is not opposed to joining the conservative cause just to make sure that blacks are represented. Cornell Hall, one of the Republican race men, shared this sentiment—both believe that it is wiser for blacks to be present in both political camps than to limit themselves to the Democratic Party alone.

Southern Customs: Faith and Individualism

Corliss Bond—Whelan University

Part of the culture of the South is grounded in religious principles that are linked to the belief that it is the moral duty of individuals to take care of themselves and their families (Black and Black 1987). Another aspect of religious belief that feeds this individualistic culture is the idea that if a person is doing "God's will," God will take care of that person. Illness and economic hardships are sometimes looked upon as the result of disobedience to God.

These are powerful cultural ideals, and they are not the exclusive domain of southern whites. Corliss Bond, a sophomore at Whelan University, embraces these ideals. She is from a small town not far from the city, and says that she chose Whelan in part because it was not very far from her home. Her father is disabled and cannot work; however, her mother is a successful businesswoman and provides well for the family. Corliss is active in many organizations on campus, including the NAACP.

This involvement with a black organization is a first for her. In middle school she "hung out with white people." When asked why, she says that "the black kids were really bad and always into things. And I mean even though I was kind of like a rebel, I wasn't into doing all the stuff they were doing." The "stuff" they were doing turned out to be using alcohol and other drugs in the school. By the time she was in high school all her friends were black. She explains this by saying that she and her white friends "just grew apart."

Corliss interjects several times during the interview to say that racism was not a factor in her community. However, the Rodney King incident made her "stop and look at things." This incident made her question her belief that racism did not exist:

> You know, I mean, you think, as far as growing up in [hometown]. It's like you really don't see a whole lot of racism and everything like that. So you know, you are kind of brought up and led to believe that racism doesn't really exist anymore. And then, you know, something like that happens and it's kind of like maybe it still does.

As the interview progresses, Corliss remembers that there was a racial incident in her community, which happened at her high school. There was a debate about the appropriateness of confederate flag shirts worn by white students, and the Malcolm X clothing worn by black students. The conflict was resolved by banning both confederate flag shirts and "X" hats and shirts. After the ban, racial slurs directed at blacks were written on the walls around the school. Corliss said that nothing was done about this and the incident just "blew over."

Corliss only thinks of what she has in common with other blacks "once in a while." She does not think her fate is linked with the fate of other blacks unless "the government somehow or other gets involved and it becomes a really big, you know, nationally advertised situation, and even then probably not a whole lot." Corliss is not entirely comfortable discussing her feelings about her racial group membership during the interview. Part of the reason may be that she believes that a black identity has to do with being poor and committing crimes. She says, "All blacks are categorized as poor, drug users, the whole nine. No one is out there trying to better themselves." Her conservatism may be linked to her desire to challenge negative images of blacks.

Interestingly, Corliss does not think of herself as a conservative— she thinks she is liberal because she does hold some liberal views. Corliss defines a conservative as someone who is "laid back." She also thinks conservatives do not want to "move forward" at all, and disapprove of homosexuality. Moderates are "taking it slowly—moving forward, but slowly." Liberals are "moving forward fast." Corliss's father is conservative and her mother is moderate. Corliss is an Independent when it comes to party affiliation, but so far has voted Republican.

Corliss is quite liberal on abortion rights, gay rights, and premarital sex; however, she does not approve of having out-of-wedlock children. She supports women's rights, which is consistent with her views on abortion. Corliss voted the Republican ticket in the 1994 midterm election, which was significant since her state had one of the most conservative Republican tickets in the country. Corliss Bond's perception of herself as a liberal is clearly at odds with the views she expressed in the interview—except in the areas of abortion and women's rights. She talked about discussions she had had with her friends on whether or not a local black man accused of a murder in their state should be extradited from another state for prosecution. Her friends do not believe he will receive a fair trial because of racism. Corliss believes that he should stand trial where the crime was committed—and accept whatever punishment is meted out.

Corliss disagrees with affirmative action, and believes that blacks do not succeed in life because "they don't try hard enough." She says the main factor in the perpetuation of black poverty and other negative conditions in the black community is the welfare system. Welfare, in Corliss's view, keeps blacks from "bettering themselves." She mentions her mother's ability to take over the support of the family since her father's disabling accident as proof that people can do better than they think. Corliss would like to see stricter limits on welfare payments, and more emphasis on education and jobs. She thinks the government is already doing its part in guaranteeing racial equality by having antidiscrimination laws. Corliss does not see a need for government to do more. Only four students out of the entire sample interviewed for this book said they believed blacks would achieve full social and economic equality in their lifetimes. Corliss Bond was one of those students.

Corliss Bond is from a closely knit family in a rural community.

The church that the family attends is nondenominational and integrated. Corliss is active in the church and it is a central part of her life. Religious faith, in part, gives Corliss the confidence that her life chances will not be compromised by her racial group membership. She also believes that her decisions will be different from those of blacks who find themselves locked out of opportunities, and that she is therefore unlikely to share their fate. Corliss observed her mother take over responsibility for the family's financial well-being by building a successful business from scratch, and she believes others could do the same. The political decisions she makes are based on these beliefs, not on positions candidates take regarding race.

Young, Wealthy, and Black

The next two students are from upper-class families, and neither has been exposed to many people, especially blacks, who are from less privileged backgrounds. In some ways they are similar: both point to the success of their parents as proof that blacks are not oppressed in this country. The parents of both are immigrants, and both attend majority-white elite institutions. There are some differences; one grew up in a large midwestern city, and the other in a midsized southern city; one has parents of African origin, while the other's parents are of West Indian origin; one is male and the other female.

West Indians, as a group, seem to fare better economically than African-Americans. This has been attributed to the confidence acquired from growing up in majority-black countries and arriving in the United States with more job experience. It is also well-known that West Indians are often critical of indigenous blacks, believing that they lack the drive and ambition for success (Foner 1987).

The conservative perspectives of these two students is partly the result of growing up in well-off communities, and partly the result of parental influence. It cannot be ignored that both sets of parents are immigrants and see the United States in much the same light as European immigrants at the turn of the century—as the land of hope and opportunity. For both families this vision has been realized, in part because both fathers came to this country already possessing an education and considerable skills. This is often the case with immigrants from developing countries. Moreover, by locating in metropolitan areas they more easily fulfill their dreams of economic security (Boston 1988). Once secure, these immigrants more fervently embrace the idea that it is possible for everyone to succeed in America—if they are willing to work hard.

Carol Changa—Woodson University

Carol Changa grew up in an upscale suburb of a midsized city in the South. She is a young woman of delicate features and manner. The offspring of parents who were born in Africa, Carol has been given many advantages and opportunities. Both parents are professionals, and her mother is an active member of the Republican Party. She had serious problems with her identity, since she went to an all-white school and her family was the only black family in the neighborhood:

> I used to think I was white. It took me a long time, probably until middle school, but I came to the realization that I was a minority. For some reason I used to flip my hair and wash my hair every day, just like white people did.[2] Used to scrub my body to get lighter—it was bad. . . . When white people would talk about niggers I would join in the laughter because I didn't consider myself colored.

Carol has very dark skin, which she scrubbed so vigorously that she nearly injured herself. Her parents decided to transfer her, in part because of these identity problems, to an all-black high school. This was a difficult transition for her. She resisted it by behaving and dressing in a manner that "would automatically [show people that] I was different and I was not one of them. So it took a lot of verbal abuse from my peers to make me find out I was a minority." This verbal abuse included calling her names like "Uncle Tom" and teasing her about her complexion by calling her "Dark Shadows." After she had accepted her membership in a minority race, Carol resented her parents for "taking away my blackness from me." She believes that only white people encourage their children to take ballet and piano lessons, and that by doing this her parents contributed to her inability to accept her racial membership. Carol now has no white friends, and associates with people from different ethnic backgrounds at Woodson.

Carol insists that she has never experienced racial discrimination, and says that "maybe it's because I'm a woman and the way I talk." Later she remembers a recent incident in which whites drove by her home and yelled at her and a younger sibling, "Get out of the neighborhood, niggers." Carol says that this incident got her "in the mode of hate all the white people." Yet she admits that all her ideas about black people came from white people. She has internalized all the stereotypes about blacks—which makes it harder to accept, even today, that she is a part of this group. According to Carol, that is why she and her parents had such a confrontational relationship in high school. She feels they had an obligation to tell her how important it is to know that you are black.

When asked about a black identity, Carol says that she believes there is one, but she doesn't think it can be defined:

> I don't think anyone can define the levels of blackness ... [or] say that Clarence Thomas is an Uncle Tom or any less black than someone who comes from the ghetto—everybody has their own—I'm sure if he had a different dialect or a different way of speaking, he wouldn't have that stigma upon him. That's like saying my father doesn't have a black identity because he's a professional.

Carol wears contact lenses that render her eyes a pale gray and hair extensions to lengthen her natural hair. Other students are critical of her because of these accessories, but Carol thinks they are being hypocritical and unfair:

> They say you're a sellout. But if you put a perm in your head, you know, you're still kind of conforming to the white man's mentality. Even though they don't see it like that—why don't you wear your hair natural? You know, don't come down on me because I want to wear a weave [the weaving in of synthetic or natural hair for length and thickness] and contacts.

When pressed for a description of herself, Carol does not include her racial membership. When the interviewer points this out, she says, "Race is very tedious to me as a description. What does that mean? . . . Blacks have to define [black identity] individually for themselves. There is no standard for blackness."

Carol's early interaction with whites and her socioeconomic status have contributed to a weak identity that she feels compelled to strengthen. Yet her political attitudes are reflective of her ideas about minorities. She believes the main factor contributing to black poverty is that blacks blame the white man for everything. She says, "They need to come of out of that state [of mind]. They say the white man won't give them a job, but first of all they don't have a college education. There is financial aid. I know plenty of people now that didn't go to college but they have a job."

Carol defines herself as a political liberal. She also thinks her mother is liberal, even though her mother is active in both state and local Republican politics. There has been one exception, when her mother worked for a Democratic candidate for Congress. Her father, she says, is definitely a conservative. She defines conservative as "outdated, close-minded, narrow-minded, racist comes to mind sometimes." She defines liberals as open-minded, but says that they can be "extremist a little bit." Moderates for Carol are somewhere in between. She sees herself as open-minded, but not extremist. In the one election in which she participated, she voted the Democratic ticket. When Carol is asked about her ideas on a variety of issues, her responses are conservative, except on abortion and homosexuality. She approves of abortion on demand, and is liberal on issues of women's rights, premarital sex, out-of-wedlock childbearing, and homosexuality. Her conservatism becomes apparent in her answers on affirmative action, welfare, and the issue of responsibility for poverty and other problems in the black community.

Carol believes affirmative action "has proven to be bad in some cases because when I first came here [to Woodson] I was told that I was only here because Woodson had a specific quota to meet." She does not believe this is true because of her exceptional grade point average and SAT scores; however, because of the stigma, she does not approve of affirmative action. She also believes welfare spending should be greatly reduced, because "A lot of people on welfare don't need to be. I've been in a situation where I've played cards, and they [food stamp recipients] will play for food stamps."

When Carol is questioned about her seemingly contradictory feelings of hatred toward whites and her conservative views on affirmative action and welfare, she replies: "I'm like my father—he hates white people and he's always in their faces." She says she is attempting to redirect her anger toward whites in more positive ways. Carol cannot explain her feelings. She says she wants her voice to be heard, that she wants whites to know that she does not like being stereotyped. The idea that whites assume all blacks are poor, or that they may steal while shopping, disturbs Carol—because she has learned that it is difficult for them to distinguish her from less fortunate blacks. At Woodson, Carol is reminded that stereotypes of blacks exist, and it makes her uncomfortable. As an example, Carol mentions a class at Woodson where the students requested help from one of the Asian students, when she was doing better in the class.

Carol feels that a stigma is attached to women who are dark complexioned, and she is not entirely mistaken. There is evidence that black women whose complexions are dark are less likely than black fairer-complexioned women to marry (Hughes and Hertel 1990). Colorism, or the tendency for blacks to treat fairer members of the race differently from darker members, is a painful but widely acknowledged problem. Spike Lee broached the subject in his film *School Daze*, in which the fairer-skinned sorority girls on the majority-black campus (the setting of the film) were "wannabes," and the darker-skinned girls were "jigaboos." In the introduction to *Black Bourgeosie*, author E. Franklin Frazier mentions that the racial pride exhibited by the black middle class was betrayed by the value placed "upon a white or light complexion" (Frazier 1957).

Carol has been taunted about her dark skin since high school. She says that when black men say to her "you look good for a black sister," it makes her angry. She believes that being fair complexioned is more important for black women than for black men, and this exacerbates her feelings of not belonging in either the black or the white community.

At the time of the interview, Carol was active in an organization whose members are trying to eliminate ethnic barriers. Carol says that blacks, whites, Asians, and Latinos are all members of this group, which she prefers to organizations such as the Black Student Alliance. She hopes this compromise will resolve her ongoing conflict regarding racial group membership and its meaning.

Some young people faced with an identity crisis resolve it by embracing black nationalism, but the rhetoric of Louis Farrakhan has turned Carol away from this philosophy. She thinks Farrakhan is a good speaker, but she finds him "funny," as in absurd. Carol believes blacks should question their political leaders more, and not allow black politicians to provide symbolic rather than substantive representation.

Carol's socioeconomic status, exposure to whites at an early age, parental influence, and finally, her majority-white environment, have resulted in a young woman with a less developed sense of racial group identity and conservative attitudes on policies that affect African-Americans. Carol's upper-middle-class status presents an extra obstacle to the successful resolution of this dilemma. In Carol's mind, most blacks are poor, which means that she has little in common with most members of her racial group. She has attempted to construct an identity that does not include racial membership as a primary component, hence her reluctance to join black organizations. The fact that her complexion works against her within the black community, especially given her gender status, makes her ambivalent about claiming membership in the race. Carol may continue to gravitate toward multiethnic organizations and causes, which is perhaps the most acceptable way to resolve her identity crisis.

Black Is a Color

Carl Franks—Windsor University

Carl Franks is the son of upper-middle-class West Indian parents. The culture of his parents, as well as the majority-white school environment, may have much to do with his traditional conservative views. The economic success of West Indian immigrants, defined here as people coming from the islands of the Caribbean, is often presented as evidence that racism is not responsible for the lack of comparable success among native black Americans (Sowell 1983).

West Indian immigrants consider themselves different from, and often superior to, black Americans because of their ties to European cultures. They want to be distinguished from native black Americans because they know that native blacks are negatively stereotyped and suffer discrimination in employment and housing. They also believe that their culture is fundamentally different—that they are more industrious and independent than native black Americans, and therefore deserve recognition as a distinct group.

The difficulty is that white Americans can see little difference between West Indians and African-Americans—especially West Indians of a darker complexion. Although dark skin is as stigmatized in the Caribbean as it is in the United States, one can overcome the disadvantages of a dark complexion by acquiring the education, manners, and economic position of mulattoes and whites. West Indians are frustrated when they discover that good manners, education, and a sophisticated manner are not enough, at least in this country, to overcome their racial group membership (Foner 1987; Stafford 1987).

As Carl speaks, he makes it clear that there are distinctions to be made among blacks. Black identity for Carl is about physical attributes and knowledge:

> I think being black is a twofold thing: it has to do with color and with pigmentation of skin, and then there are different shades of gray in this whole thing—because I know some very light-skinned blacks who look almost white. OK. But they are very black . . . but also, knowledge of a culture, history, and knowledge of what your perception is in this country, how you are perceived in this country.

Growing up in a middle-class community, Carl had an opportunity to meet a number of successful blacks. Watching and listening to these people—politicians, professionals, and businessmen—taught him that accomplished blacks did not focus on race. He was disappointed in the campaign of a black candidate for office in his city who commented that more blacks were needed in government:

I'm like why would you want to delve into, to play the race card or delve into the race card? By doing that, I mean I know Reginald Lewis[3] said this in his book, colors and labels have a tendency to place artificial limits on you. I mean I read that and I took it to heart. That kind of summed up what I was thinking. A lot of these people that are doing these things, doing the high-up things, the things they want to do, didn't let colors or labels put any kind of limits on them. Where you hear the other guys talking about yeah, you know, the man talking about this, and that the white man's this, and the white man's that, and the white man keeps me down, and the man—and I'm like, the only man keeping you down is yourself.

Carl says that he hardly ever thinks about being black, but believes that what happens generally to blacks will affect him a lot. He says that if affirmative action is rescinded on a large scale it will definitely affect him, but it will not prevent him from being successful. The subject of racial solidarity is a sensitive one for him at the moment, because there has been disagreement among the black students during the year about the importance of black unity.

Carl explains that one of the ways student leaders tried to smooth over the dispute was to stage a "Unity Step Show." "Stepping" is a display of choreographed routines by black fraternities and sororities. These routines are often dazzling, with intricate formations and transitions. The "Unity Step Show" would have featured black Greeks and Independents "stepping" together. He disagreed with this idea:

> And we talked about the thing about the black community uh, being unified. And I said I don't believe the black community—I don't believe in black unity because I'm learning that things in this world are not about black and white. It's about the spirit that people have. This is my spirituality starting to grow and mature. And when you limit yourself to just black people you're doing a great disservice to yourself. And this started from me this last summer being here and getting to know some white people in my classes where before I would never speak to them—never say any words to them. I don't believe in black unity because we're not all about the same thing. I don't believe that we should have some kind of unity and I should look out for people just because we have the same color. Because it does not mean we're about the same ideals or the same things. I mean I could see a brother

walking down the street, you know, and say I should have black unity with this man. But that man could run out and rob people. And I have nothing in common with that man and don't want to have anything in common with him. We happen to both be black. I mean, that type deal. I'm learning, and that's something my father has tried to instill in me, is that don't look at color first, look at other things first. Be an American who happens to be black, don't be a black American. If you see what I'm saying about the difference.

Carl was asked if he had ever experienced racism. He said no, and added, "I'm not one to call racism at the drop of a dime. I don't do that." He said he went to look for an apartment in the area and landlords assumed he was from Benedict, the historically black college in the area. Although he said that some people might think that assumption was racist, he did not. He thought it was logical because the percentage of blacks at Windsor is so low that that sort of assumption makes sense.

For Carl, a conservative is someone who is white and right-wing. Conservatives, in his view, believe in self-help, small government, and "in being judged on the basis of numerical facts and not based on taking outside factors into account." He also believes that conservatives are religious fundamentalists. Moderates have mixed views—some are liberal, others are conservative. Liberals are "left, out the box." Carl identifies liberals with being supportive of big government:

> People who believe in big government and government should help everybody. Government should be above everything. They don't like business. They don't like small enterprise. People who are just crazy out the box. People who are more caught up in color, I think. Conservatives are more based on numbers, on the facts, who's the best, who's number one—whereas liberals are always caught up in color—what's white, what's gray—all this and all that.

When asked about the ideological leanings of his parents, Carl says his father is a moderate conservative. Carl's father and male siblings are entrepreneurs, and his mother is a homemaker. He does not know how his mother feels about political issues: "Me and my Mom don't talk about things like that. When it comes to my political views, my Dad pretty much formed them. My Mom gave me a concept of morality about things. My Dad helped me form my political views about things."

Carl names the lack of a solid family structure and an extended family, drugs, self-centeredness, and reliance on government as the main problems in the black community. He believes that the legalization of drugs is the first step in solving these problems. Legalized drugs, welfare reform, and "religion back in the schools" will deter crime. Carl's family is devoutly religious, and he believes that this is the key to success. His logic is that if religious principles were adhered to, many problems would be eliminated. There would be fewer children born out-of-wedlock and more marriages. Drug usage would be reduced, which would automatically reduce crime. Carl completed the statement, "In the United States, if black people don't do well in life, it is because . . . " with the following: "First of all they don't have God in their life; because they are not humble; and they limit themselves."

Carl supports affirmative action, but would like to see it based on the premise that anyone deprived of an adequate education should receive special consideration. He thinks the welfare system discourages people from working, but believes government should ensure fairness in the job market.

Carl is pro-choice on abortion, but hopes that people will choose life. He says that he is "very intolerant" of homosexual behavior, but "very tolerant" of homosexuals. He does not think children should be born outside marriage, and is lukewarm on the question of women having careers. Carl's objection to the economic independence of women is that it is wrong from a biblical standpoint. He does not think all women should be homemakers, but says that "there can be only one captain of a ship, and men should serve in that role in the home."

Carl Franks is reminiscent of Charles Gaston, one of the Republican race men at Brooks. Both have West Indian parents, and strong influential fathers. However, Carl does not share Charles's feelings of obligation to other blacks or his admiration for Louis Farrakhan.

Carl perceives Farrakhan as someone who takes advantage of blacks, saying, "He's a con man. He's a con man. He is the ultimate con man. . . . His views and the Nation of Islam's views—a lot of them on self-help and black empowerment I believe—but other than that, he's a con man."

The life experiences of Carl Franks have led him to believe in the primacy of merit and hard work as the prescription for economic woes. In his view, the race problem stems from an overreliance on race as an explanation for individual failure. He believes that his father and his father's friends have demonstrated that race need not be a factor in determining success in life. Placing the responsibility for problems squarely on the shoulders of blacks themselves, Carl Franks is poised to enter the world with all the privileges that he is sure will be the reward for being fundamentalist and financially secure.

Summary

With the exception of Carl Franks, these traditional conservatives identify themselves as Independents. (Carl did not claim any partisan identity.) They cannot align themselves with Democrats for a variety of reasons. For some, it is the Democrats' liberal stance on abortion and tolerance of alternative lifestyles. For others, it is a perception that Democrats favor too many social programs. The Republican Party has alienated most blacks with its anti-affirmative action rhetoric—not to mention the memory of the Willie Horton ads of the 1988 Bush presidential campaign.

All these students are from two-parent households, as were the Republican race men. Carol Changa and Carl Franks are similar to the Republican race men in that they name their fathers as the most influential people in their lives. Carol's characterization of her father's influence is not completely positive, but he was frequently mentioned during the interview as an example of how successful blacks can be in this country. There seems to be a connection between socioeconomic status, traditional households, and traditional attitudes. Most of the moderate students in the next chapter are also from middle-class families. They differ from the traditional conservatives in that they have a strong sense of racial group identity, yet hold a range of conservative and liberal ideas about what this identity means for their life chances.

4

Issues of Empowerment and Liability
The Moderates

Several strands connect the six students who hold more moderate political attitudes: First, all but one are solidly middle class; second, they have not experienced much discrimination; third, all but two attend majority-white institutions; and fourth, all point to the failure of both blacks and whites to solve racial problems. Of the six students, only one is from an urban setting, and three are from single-parent families. This group is the smallest among the interviewees, and, along gender lines, it is the most evenly divided: three women and three men.

The individualist perspective dominates the views of these moderate students. While the racial group identities of most are strong to moderate, these identities are grounded in the more positive aspects of treating other blacks with respect and acknowledging a common history, rather than the negative aspects of discrimination. Three of the six feel that there is no black identity to speak of, and that it may be dangerous to attempt to define such a thing. The danger lies in reducing the black experience to stereotypes, exacerbating an already severe problem. Several of the students who grew up in the South worry about the way blacks are perceived by the larger public, and believe blacks should comport themselves in more socially acceptable ways. In sum, the views of these students represent the ways in which integration, education, and increased media exposure to politics and contemporary social issues have influenced the post–civil rights generation.

The Stigma of Inferiority: Pressure to Perform

Marie Potter—Woodson University

Marie Potter, a student from a large northeastern city, is a sophisticated young woman with a mature presence. She grew up in an all-black neighborhood, and attended an all-black elementary school. She is from a single-parent home, although her father is a strong presence in her life. Marie's mother is a professional, and active politically and socially. Her father is also a professional, and, with her mother, has seen to it that Marie received exceptional educational opportunities.

Marie attended a high school with a special curriculum designed to attract a diverse student body—a "magnet" school. This was her first integration experience. This high school had no formal grading system, which helped Marie to focus more on learning. At first Marie liked and was comfortable in this new school setting. As one of the few blacks attending, this began to change in her second year, when she experienced some "difficulty." She was vague about the nature of this "difficulty," but indicated that it was just a generalized feeling of not belonging. This is when she began to think about attending a historically black university, which indicates that her difficulty was racial in nature. This desire to be in an all-black environment emerged when "all my friends I still hung out with were the ones I knew from before and they were black. I didn't get integrated into the population at the school. I didn't get into any of the cliques." In other words, Marie was not accepted as part of the student body, and her social life remained as circumscribed as it had been before she came to the school. The relationships she had formed with the black students in the all-black school from which she transferred sustained her in the new majority-white environment.

This period in her life serves as a reference point when she comments on what she feels binds blacks to one another in ways that other groups are not similarly bound:

> We're all in the same boat. We're all here, especially at this university, to prove ourselves. To say that, "yes, we can handle anything that you throw at us and still come out at the same level as another person." I

really have to be ten steps ahead of the people that I graduate with in order to be at the same level as them when I'm job searching. I have to have at least three or four work experiences. They just come out of Woodson with one internship and get that job. But I have to have a whole lot more experience and corporate background behind me to be in the same running with them for that position.

Marie also feels that black identity is related to a first-hand knowledge of the effects of inequality and cultural differences:

[You] have experienced the inequities due to having to—being a member of another race, or being less superior than another. And not being able—not benefiting from all the opportunities that they can because, you know—there is also black culture. The familial ties are close. And even if you're not family, you can be family. There is no real division between that ... there's a caring ... that all-inclusive thing. To me, like if a black person sees another person who is having a hard time, you know, down all the time or don't know how to do some-thing—they will actually reach out and help them. They will nurture them. No matter who that person is just because it's in their nature to reach out.

Marie feels pressure in this university setting to perform better than her white peers. She believes that other black students feel it too, and that they share the anxieties brought on by this pressure. This com-mon condition is what helps black people create familial ties in unfa-miliar or unfriendly environs.

Although Marie mentioned her difficulty in high school, when she is asked whether she has ever experienced racial discrimination, she answers "no." She thinks, however, that her uncle may have when he was arrested in a case of mistaken identity. When she relates the story, she emphasizes that she is "not sure it was racial." Later she says:

I had a couple of friends, guys really, guys I knew really had hard times with police brutality and this whole harassment thing. And I know people even down here, I know guys who hate white people. Don't like them at all. And, I can understand it. Even now I can understand where they are coming from but I still can't understand how you can hate all white people. But that gets me thinking.

Marie defines herself as a moderate to liberal person ideologically. She defines a conservative as "probably pro-life, or Republicans. Their children go to private schools; they are well-to-do; they are probably in corporate America. Don't like taxes, not into a lot of, not into social funding, funding of social programs." Liberals, on the other hand, "want all the programs." Liberals try to change things, and favor taxing the rich to pay for programs for the poor. Marie believes poverty and crime in the black community are the result of a substandard education. She uses her own experience as an example:

> Something that I have been able to compare going from public to private—and especially in the city—this is what I know. In my city, you cannot come out of public school socially ready to function in this society. You just don't have the background. You don't have it.

Although Marie thinks the government should spend more on education, she has doubts about the power of government to change things. She states that the government cannot guarantee racial equality; furthermore, individuals must have the desire for a better life: "Once you get [to] a certain age you have to want the education—and how do you get that into—how do you instill the want inside of someone? That's what I'm trying to work on or trying to figure out." She also believes the cooperation of parents is essential in this process, but understands that this might be difficult to arrange.

Like most of the young people interviewed, Marie does not admire any contemporary African-American political (elected) leader. She does, however, respect Louis Farrakhan. Farrakhan is "doing something to help." Islam is a good thing, because "for us, spirituality and life go hand-in-hand. And when you separate the two, and the American way has been pretty much separated, you know, we lack the ability to function. You put the two together and you give people goals to strive for." Marie is not interested in becoming a member of the Nation of Islam herself, but she believes it offers many blacks in the cities a way out of crime and drug addiction.

Marie Potter was placed in an integrated environment in high school, when many aspects of her ethnic identity were already firmly in place. Woodson, she says, reminds her of her high school experience in that she does not feel a part of that institution's culture either. She does have one white friend, with whom she shares a dislike of the South (they are from the same city) and extracurricular interests. Marie cannot relate any experiences with racism, even though her experiences in high school indicate that her "difficulty" may have been discrimination. She notes that a number of her male friends seem to have had many encounters with racism. It is also possible that the kind of racism faced by Marie is more subtle and slippery than the kind faced by her male friends. Marie is certain that blacks as a group have a connection that is akin to familial ties, and talks more about "not belonging" than about racism. Most importantly, Marie believes, as does the next student, that ultimately the desire to achieve must come from within.

Controlling Fate by Doing the Right Thing

Marilyn Lacey—Whelan University

Marilyn is the only child of a single parent, and believes that her values and hard work will determine her circumstances. She maintains that she has never felt deprived in any way as the child of a single parent. She was raised in the Northeast in a small town and attended several schools—some were integrated and others were not. She is a petite woman who was meticulously dressed for work at the time of the interview.

Marilyn "hardly ever" thinks about what she has in common with other blacks. When she was asked when she first became aware that she was black and that it made a difference to some people, she says it was around the first grade. She was then attending an all-black school. When they had a black history month, she learned a lot about black history that she did not know. However, she says she did not realize that people may treat you differently because you are black until the Rodney King incident, which happened during her first year in college. Marilyn also mentions that in discussions of the O. J. Simpson trial, she has taken the position that if the victim had been a black woman the trial would not have received as much publicity because "there is a value placed on people and people's lives. By her being a white woman I think there is a little higher value placed on her living or dying than maybe an African-American woman living or dying."

Marilyn does not believe there is any such thing as a black identity. She is also uncertain that her fate is linked to the fate of other blacks, saying "sometimes I guess I do, but sometimes I don't." Her heart sometimes tells her that she may be subjected to the same fate as less fortunate blacks, but her head denies it. Marilyn comes in contact with a lot of poor young black women on her job. She says when she sees and talks with these women, it reminds her that she has little in common with them although they are members of the same race. She was asked if she thought she could ever be treated the way Rodney King was. Her answer was that if she worked hard and obeyed the law, she expected never to be in a situation where "certain things can happen to me."

Marilyn was asked whether she had ever been involved in an incident that she felt was racially charged. She recalled something that had happened in a grocery store parking lot after her second year in college. A vicious dog in the back of a truck attempted to attack Marilyn and her mother. The owner returned to his truck in time to prevent the attack, but when Marilyn complained to him about the dog, he called her a "black bitch" and threatened to allow the dog to attack her. She says that this "may have been a racial incident"—but she is not sure.

Marilyn has a simple way of thinking about political attitudes. Conservatives, moderates, and liberals are distinguished only by their degree of openness. Conservatives are less open (meaning less open-minded), moderates are willing to listen, and liberals are "really open," and willing to listen to every side of the issue. She considers herself moderate to liberal, and says that her mother is the same. One thing that has influenced her ideas on politics was the election of an African-American to high office in her state. When the African-American won office, people thought that things would change for the better. But they found that things remained the same.

It made Marilyn think about whether blacks necessarily represent black interests: "An African-American isn't always the right [person], you know, I mean, it can be, but you know it depends on what the person stands for and what the person does when they get in there. You have to really look at the candidate and see what their track record is."

Marilyn believes problems in the black community result from a lack of education and jobs. The solution is to have programs that keep people in school. However, Marilyn says if blacks do not succeed in life, it is because "opportunities were not available to them or they didn't take advantage of opportunities that were available to them." She thinks that the role of government in ensuring racial equality is simply to ensure that everyone has an equal opportunity for success. Marilyn supports affirmative action only if it can be demonstrated that it is necessary: "it wouldn't be necessary to even give special consideration if we knew that equal consideration would be given to all candidates. If that were the case [each candidate receiving equal consideration], I would disagree [with affirmative action]."

Marilyn says that the federal government is spending too much on welfare, and should spend more on education and crime. She says that if a person can work, he or she should do so:

> [You should not] sit back and let the state take care of you. I say that because I've had like family members that have received welfare at one time in their life. And they like got in a program and things of that nature. And I mean now they are working—and if they can do it, why can't you—why can't other people do it? It'll make it a little bit less expensive on taxpayers. Also it would help society as a whole, you know, when somebody, if you are out working, and you know, working for a living. Then you would feel better about yourself.

Liberal on most moral and cultural issues such as abortion and homosexuality, Marilyn has always voted the Democratic ticket. Her moderate ideology is more apparent in the way she views black issues such as welfare and affirmative action. Marilyn feels that there are no African-American leaders today, and she is not enamored of Louis Farrakhan. She says she cannot relate to any of Farrakhan's ideas. According to Marilyn, the one time she listened to Farrakhan in a television address, he was sexist in his remarks:

> . . . he was talking to a group of black women I believe. And you know, and he was just making the assumption that all black women [were being] beaten or had been beaten by spouses and hit. And I was like that's not necessarily the case. Some of the things he said was like, made women feel like they were second class, you know, second class citizens. I just didn't like that.

Marilyn Lacey is from a small community with few blacks in residence. She has had few experiences that she believes are related to race. Marilyn is not religious; therefore her confidence that things will work out is not related to religious faith. However, she feels in control of her destiny because she is making decisions and planning her life so that it unfolds to her liking. The feeling that race is not as significant as hard work and planning is supported by the example set by Marilyn's mother. Her weak racial identity, which may come from the majority of her growing up years being spent in majority-white schools and neighborhoods, has not been strengthened by her attendance at Whelan University—perhaps because of Whelan's lack of racial tension. Her views on affirmative action, which is a group benefit, are perhaps influenced by her weak identity. It may also influence her view that people who can work should work because she does not perceive that the group is being systematically oppressed. For example, although she says that black problems are caused by lack of education and jobs, she also believes that education is obtained by individual effort.

The Accountability of the Media and the Middle Class

Michael Washington—Whelan University

Several of the students interviewed talked extensively about the role of the middle class in improving the lives of poorer blacks. They were also critical of media images, and believed that the portrayal of blacks, particularly of black men, is largely to blame for whites' negative views of blacks. Michael Washington, from a small rural community not far from Whelan, is one of those students. Michael's mother is a homemaker and his father is a skilled laborer. His memories of childhood are pleasant, although his family struggled financially for a time. He remains active in his home church, and believes it is important to show "what God has done in my life."

Michael thinks about being black fairly often, and reminds me that *Plessy v Ferguson*[1] is proof that what happens to one African-American can affect the entire population. When asked if he could define a black identity, Michael replied that "every African-American can identify with Jim Crow and racism. Experiences with discrimination bind all blacks."

Michael believes he experienced racism when he entered high school. Teachers and counselors placed him in vocational classes although he had been on an academic track in middle school. He says "I wondered how in the world this could have happened to me" when he found himself in one vocational class after another. Michael noticed that these classes were all-black, although at the time he did not connect this with any intention on the part of school administrators to discourage black men from going to college. According to Michael, his parents intervened: "They weren't dealing with dummies. My parents came to the school and said no, our son is on a cp/ap [college preparatory/advanced placement] track." His schedule was promptly changed, but he was the only black in the cp/ap classes.

Michael also recalls an incident in which a friend of his, a high-ranking navy officer, was stopped and harassed on the interstate by police. He says that his friend told him "no matter what you do, I mean it doesn't matter, if a brother is driving a nice car, if they're in a suit, if they have a nice job, a nine-to-five job, it still doesn't free you. You're still going to be harassed." Michael has an idea of how whites see African-American males:

> White America, they have this image of African-American males. Pants hanging to their knees, carrying nine millimeters, out here on Main Street selling crack. And so they perceive that if you're a brother driving a nice car then you must be a criminal. I heard from somewhere, I believe it was Les Brown,[2] that it is actually probably less than

2 percent of our population. It bothers me that a majority of our people are being described by the acts of a minority.

Michael describes a conservative as having a closed mind and not being open to new ideas. Conservatives want to maintain the status quo or return to the way things used to be. A moderate sits on both sides of the fence, and a liberal is "very open and willing to try anything." Michael considers his father moderate to conservative, his mother liberal, and himself "strictly moderate."

The source of problems in the black community, in Michael's view, comes from a lack of education. The only way this problem can be solved is by successful blacks returning to the black community and teaching young blacks how to finance a college education. Michael believes that many poor blacks are not aware of financial aid and grants. This lack of knowledge about the process of college admissions is a major obstacle. He adds, however, that he also believes some blacks use lack of funding as an excuse for not attending college.

Michael and his friends have recently been discussing affirmative action. He is not sure that affirmative action is a good idea:

> The one article that I read in *Newsweek* was about this brother out in California who owns 50 percent of a business. The other 50 percent of the business is owned by his wife. And his wife is Caucasian. He was discussing in this article how affirmative action should be done away with because if he owned 51 percent of the business, he doesn't want to be known as an affirmative action business owner. That sticks in my mind. I can see his opinion on that. I don't think America is ready to do away with it yet . . . technically we're still behind. And I think that [abolishing affirmative action] would push us further behind.

Michael says that when you are a recipient of affirmative action, people do not give you credit for your accomplishments. You are seen as a person who was given an opportunity because you are black. While Michael is ambivalent about affirmative action, he believes that supporting such programs is the responsibility of the government. Government has an obligation to help level the playing field, and supporting affirmative action policies is a means of fulfilling that obligation.

Michael thinks government should decrease social security payments and increase funding for education. He agrees with efforts to reform welfare, and approves the two-year limit suggested by some legislators. Michael is a registered Democrat and voted the straight Democratic ticket when he participated in his first major election. He has also worked in the campaigns of Democratic candidates for the governorship and the senate. He admires Douglas Wilder and Colin Powell, both moderates. Regarding Louis Farrakhan and the Nation of Islam, Michael says:

> They're very helpful. They're even getting government projects because it's been proven that after they put the Fruit of Islam* in the housing projects crime goes down. And these brothers aren't carrying guns or anything like that. They do a lot of positive work. I feel that as an African-American—even America as a whole—we need to respect Minister Farrakhan as a leader, because he is that.

Michael Washington has a moderately strong identity that is tempered by his religiosity and his upbringing in a small community. He is patriotic—mentioning on several occasions his pride in his state and his country. The leadership positions he holds at Whelan University are evidence to him that you can retain your racial group identity and serve the majority-white student body at the same time. Michael has political aspirations, and intends to follow the example set by Douglas Wilder and Colin Powell, two African-American political figures who have avoided being exclusively characterized by their racial group membership.

Looking Within: Black Solutions to Black Problems

Matthew Moore—Whelan University

One of Michael's fellow officers in the Student Government Association disagrees with him vehemently on the subject of Farrakhan. Matthew Moore is a tall, thin, serious young man with an urbane

---

* The Fruit of Islam is the unarmed paramilitary security force of the Nation of Islam.

quality that makes him appear out of place in this southern setting. Matthew is one of the few students who expressed doubts about Farrakhan's integrity as a leader.

Matthew has moved around a bit with his mother, who is an upwardly mobile career woman. Most of his years were spent in a small northeastern town with few blacks. He experienced integration at an early age, and first became aware of the significance of racial membership in junior high school. This awareness came about only because he was the only black in all his classes. In high school, Matthew was the only black at most of the parties he attended. He said that "something would always keep me back from having too much fun [at the parties]—and it was race. It was because I was the only black. . . . Somewhere inside of me there was a voice saying that 'you don't belong here.'" It bothered Matthew that the other black students seemed not to want his company. He speculates that it was because he was a high achiever, which placed him in all-white classes.

Matthew believes that black identity has to do with the way other blacks perceive you. He tells me that in high school he was not perceived as black; therefore, he did not have a black identity. When asked why the perception of other blacks is a good litmus test for black identity, Matthew said:

> I can give you . . . examples. We have a security guard who is very dark skinned yet he acts whiter than a lot of white people. He does not identify with us at all. If we ask him for anything, like I asked him for some change one time . . . and he was like, "I can't do that." Normally if someone white asked him that, he would probably say yes. He did have the quarters. I do know that 'cause he did say he did. And he's darker than I am. He's darker than many blacks.

> *And so you think because of these incidents of unfriendliness on [his] part that [he doesn't] have a black identity?*

> I don't think he has a strong identity.

> *Are you saying that black identity entails some loyalty to other members of your race?*

> Yes, it does.

And you demonstrate that loyalty how?
By how you treat them.

Matthew does not think about what he has in common with blacks as much as he once did simply because he is now sure of his identity: "as I've grown up and become more confident in myself I believe I know what it is to be a strong African-American male. So, I have more confidence in that, so I don't really need to think about it per se the way I used to." He wants other blacks to become more involved in the community and to help other young black men. When he was asked what became of the close friendships he had developed in high school with whites, Matthew said that part of the reason they had faded away was that they have different interests now. The other part is that they simply have no opportunities to see each other.

Matthew says that he has experienced racial discrimination from his supervisor on his work-study job because "she's frightened of black people." He believes that this fear accounts for her tendency to assign manual labor duties to the black male work-study students. Matthew says he was the exception to this rule. His assignments involved work on computers. When he was assigned to work for a politically conservative black male administrator, his work doubled. He complained to the supervisor, who refused to reassign him, which was not the usual practice in these situations. Matthew believed that she resented the fact that he had escaped manual labor duties because of his skills—and had therefore decided to force him into a position that would result in his resignation.

Matthew and his friends have been discussing the plight of black people in recent weeks, particularly the plight of the African-American male. He says the gist of the conversations is as follows:

> From my point of view it's more or less that they need to get their act together and stop blaming white people so much. A white person might knock you down, but you're the person that's keeping you there. And other ones [his friends] feel that that's not the case, or it may not be the only case, but they could also blame it on whites more so than I would.

Matthew says that he is a political moderate, and defines a moderate as "not that different from a Republican." Conservatives are "very constricted—very tight." Liberals are "free spirits—people who want to give other people all kinds of rights that aren't exactly—that the American people aren't ready for—too much freedom." Matthew is an Independent, but voted for Clinton in the 1992 presidential election.

The governor of the state, a conservative Republican, has helped shape his political attitudes. According to Matthew, "He's [the governor] taking away from education to build prisons. And if you ask me, who's going to be in those prisons—other than blacks? He's taking away from education, which is the key to getting people and keeping them out of prison. I see him as the kind of politician that you cannot trust." When Matthew is asked whether or not the government spends too much, too little, or the right amount on crime, he answers too little. He would like to see additional policemen hired so that criminal activity is discouraged.

Matthew believes that a lack of education is to blame for problems of inner-city blacks. He thinks the government should spend less money on foreign aid, and more money on education. The government is responsible for ensuring racial equality—bolstering education and punishing acts of discrimination.

A lack of education is also to blame if blacks do not succeed in life—although Matthew adds that even without an education most people could do better if they tried harder. When asked about welfare, he expresses some ambivalence. Matthew says he has known people who had children just to receive a welfare check. He thinks that people should receive help if they are truly needy; however, he thinks that people should make an effort to help themselves before seeking help from the government.

He is pro-choice on abortion with certain qualifications, and moderately tolerant on issues of gay rights and premarital sex. Matthew laughs at the question about having out-of-wedlock children and says, "I can't be too intolerant because I was conceived outside of marriage." Matthew thinks women play an important role in our society:

> The role of black women is very important, unfortunately because a
> lot of black males are not around to take care of their kids. The mother

has to be the backbone. My family is like that, is run by the women. I was raised by women. I really didn't have a male role model.

Matthew names Douglas Wilder as the black politician he admires most. However, he believes there is no dominant figure in contemporary black politics: "I really don't know of any particular one. No one has taken that vanguard position. In a way I think that's good. There shouldn't be just one person. There should be millions of us for other people to look up to." Matthew agrees with Martin Luther King, Jr., that in order for blacks to obtain justice in society, "we have to be right in the eyes of God." This is his objection to Louis Farrakhan, who he thinks returns "evil for evil." Matthew says the Nation of Islam has done some positive things, but it has problems:

> Although I would have to say that they have done a lot to improve the African-American society, I can't condone building it on the backs of white people or hatred for white people. That's reverse discrimination. That's doing to them what they did to us. And that would make us no better than them. And that's wrong.

Matthew Moore's weak racial identity has been transformed into a strong one by attending college in the South and increased contact and interaction with other blacks. In the process, his sense of responsibility for helping less fortunate blacks has developed. However, because he perceives that hard work is an important factor in determining one's life chances, he believes that what happens to blacks generally may only affect his life "some." Matthew believes that individuals have the power to overcome adversity. This may be because he witnessed his mother change his family's socioeconomic status from lower-to-working class to middle-to-upper class by educating herself, having the courage to relocate for better opportunities, and through consistent effort. In addition, he says that since he arrived at Whelan University, his religious faith has "grown considerably." This faith, in combination with Matthew's confidence in his intellectual ability and the traditional values instilled in him by his mother and grandmother, makes him less likely to blame whites or the government for problems in the African-American community.

Morgan Stone—Benedict University

Morgan expresses ideas that are reminiscent of the Brooks College men. He has a much higher degree of racial group consciousness than most of the moderate or conservative students, but is not particularly liberal in his political views. A dedicated student of political science, Morgan Stone has lived all over the country. He is active on campus and in the community, and has plans to be a political leader. Morgan's father was in the military and his mother did not work much while he was growing up. His parents took him and his siblings on extended vacations every year, and he "did not feel deprived in any way." Because of experiences such as family vacations Morgan believes he has had more advantages than many of his fellow students.

Morgan grew up with a father who often spoke about racial issues and dispensed advice on how to avoid being a victim of discrimination. He says his parents "made sure that he understood he was black." Morgan once overheard his father cautioning his older brother against dating white women—they might claim rape if the relationship ended, which would mean a life cut short by a prison term. His father also warned Morgan and his brothers about the danger of being prematurely promoted on a job, a tactic employed by whites to set blacks up for failure. Morgan's father, who was raised in the rural South, told him and his siblings stories about being taken out of school to work in the fields. These stories and conversations have given Morgan a strong sense of racial group identity.

However, this identity is not vested in a particular vision of blackness. Morgan answers "I don't care" to the question of whether he would prefer to be called black, African-American, or something else. However, he thinks about being black "a whole lot" and says that what happens to other blacks will affect him "a lot." Interestingly, Morgan thinks that defining a black identity may not be a good idea:

> You have to be careful when you say black identity, because there are a lot of different segments within the black community. My upbringing is very different from a lot of my frat [fraternity] brothers. I grew up in a very privileged environment. I have a frat brother who didn't. Blacks have a common history, and that's what brings them together.

But if you say there is a black identity, then you help justify stereotypes, and you don't want to do that. You know, you don't want to do
that because people are not shaped by the color of their skin. They are
shaped by the environment they're brought up in.

This statement typifies Morgan's thoughtful approach to racial issues,
which seems to be balanced between a keen awareness of discrimination and a commitment to honesty regarding his own experiences
and observations. Morgan cannot relate any direct experience with
racism but adds, "I have but it's been so subtle that I couldn't give you
any details." He later says that a white person once called him a "nigger," and he responded by striking the person. Despite Morgan's limited exposure to racism, he sees contemporary politics through a dis-
tinctly racial lens.

The 1994 Republican Revolution has affected Morgan's perception
of what being "conservative" means. Morgan states unequivocally that
conservatives are against the agenda of minorities. He says he thinks
of the Republican Party when he hears the word conservative, but he
knows that this is not fair. Morgan acknowledges that not all Republicans are against the minority agenda. Moderates are politicians such
as Bill Clinton and Richard Gephardt. Liberals are a dying breed—in
fact, the only liberal he can think of is Marian Wright Edelman of the
Children's Defense Fund, whom he admires: "She's still holding on to
her old views which is good. 'Cause I was very impressed with the way
she conducted herself with Ted Koppel of the *Nightline* show."

Morgan and his friends have been talking about the Republican
"Contract with America" and what they believe to be the passivity of
minorities in this country:

It's like they're being slaughtered—they're like sheep in the slaughter
and they don't even realize what's happening to them, and it's frustrating. Not so much with the average—with the community itself,
but even on college, you know. You have voting . . . you have voting
polls right there at the library. It takes no more than a second to vote
and yet, out of 5,000 students you're only going to get 632!

Morgan believes that since political attitudes are derived from parents, parents are to blame for students' disinterest in politics. He com-

ments that his parents' generation was so active that it is disappointing for him to be part of a generation apathetic about political issues. When he was asked to complete the sentence, "In the United States, if black people don't do well in life it is because," Morgan's answer indicates that he does not believe it is the individual's fault:

> One, no one instilled in them a sense of self. They allowed their dreams to die at an early age so that when they moved forward, when they were moving up in the educational system, they didn't care. Because no one cared about them. No one encouraged them. No one enriched their lives.

Morgan believes that problems in the black community stem from a lack of education: "It really boils down to education overall. Because if someone is educated, they can always move forward because they want to move forward. That's what education does for you." Organizations such as black fraternities need to "reevaluate their goals and objectives." He says they should concentrate on bringing in members with a social conscience—those who will volunteer at Boys Clubs and other community-based organizations. He is disgusted because he sees more white young men from Windsor volunteering in the community than from Benedict. Morgan wants the black community to take more responsibility:

> When are we going to realize that you cannot expect those persons who put you in these situations to get you out? Because if they could get you out, if they wanted you out, they would not have put you there in the first place. You know, we need to—I blame a lot of the problems in our community on ourselves. That's why Malcolm X got so frustrated. Because he realized how far we really had to go.

Morgan supports affirmative action and believes the government's responsibility toward blacks is simply not to promote divisions among ethnic groups. He believes that the Republican "Contract with America" divides people. Morgan thinks government spending on welfare and crime is "about right," and indicates that he is well aware that these issues are related to race. On moral and cultural issues, Morgan's views are mixed. Premarital sex and having children out-of-wedlock is "religiously wrong," although he supports women's rights.

Morgan is a registered Democrat but thinks of himself as an Independent. He voted for Clinton in 1992 because Bush was "out of touch with society" and he wanted change. Clinton's background was important to Morgan—"he understood what it meant to be poor and he was from the South." He admires Ben Chavis, the former president of the NAACP, and says that "I think he made a big mistake, but his vision was on the mark."[3] He is not sure what he thinks of Louis Farrakhan—he can only say that the Nation of Islam is positive, but adds with a laugh, "I am not sure how much they are helping themselves while they are helping the community."

Morgan Stone is committed to the idea of the collective responsibility of all blacks to help those who are in need. He is not an individualist, which is why the Republican Revolution left him disappointed and frustrated with the political process. He has been influenced by both his father's experiences growing up in the South, and his father's advice and views on negotiating his way in a white world. His father is a part-time minister, which is why his attitudes on moral and cultural issues are traditionally conservative. Morgan's views on black identity, whom he blames for black problems, and how he thinks solutions will be found is what makes him a moderate. He blames black problems on a lack of education, but believes the black community is responsible for changing that condition. Morgan would be a Republican race man were it not for his coolness toward Louis Farrakhan and the Nation of Islam. He is somewhere between the Republican race men of the first chapter, and the liberal students in the next chapter.

Sublimation of a Dual Identity

Myra Mason—Whelan University

Myra Mason is the daughter of an Asian mother and an African American father. Since her father was in the military, Myra has also spent a number of years overseas, which delayed her realization of what her mixed-race heritage would mean in the United States. She realized who "her people" were when she met her father's mother, who looked like her. This identification was strengthened when she moved to the United States at the age of seventeen. Media coverage of racial issues and the treatment she received from salesclerks when shopping in stores clued her into the existing perceptions of black people:

> It just seemed that everything that happened that was criminally related—they would always say that a black person did it or a black mother was crying on the television screen . . . . I couldn't believe that we were being treated this way, number one, and then number two that we were allowing them to do it. When I went to high school, it seemed that everyone was trying to fit in the roles that the media was portraying. The males seemed as though they wanted to dress in the way that the media was saying all black males on drugs or [in gangs] [would dress]. Some were involved in the same drug-dealing that the media said they were—and I knew they were middle-income children. I knew that no one was put in a situation where they had to wear these kinds of clothes or they had to sell drugs because they didn't have enough money. I had just come from a school where your academics [established] your status in school. If you were a good student, everyone knew that. To see us become what the media portrayed was so shocking.

When Myra shopped, she was followed, especially when she was "dressed down." She was offended by salespeople always assuming that she wanted to see the sale racks or purchase items through a payment plan.

Myra thinks about being black often, and believes that what happens to other blacks in this country will affect her a lot. She likes the term "black" because it has more of an "international connotation." Her mother emphasized to her and her brother that they would be considered black in the United States:

> My mother is from an aboriginal tribe, so her people are natives. When my grandmother met my father, she wasn't influenced by any western ideas—she just thought this is someone who is a little darker than we are. And that's it, that's the extent of it. We were welcomed into the family. But it seems like Asian culture, and I hate to generalize, but they

seem to emphasize purity. Even in Asian-American culture, you'll find that there are two tiers of the Asian community. There are the Asians that are maybe white or have white husbands or whatever. But then there is an Asian community in the States that know all the way back to China [who] their ancestors are. And if you don't have a Chinese last name, they don't accept you. Within the Asian-American community in the United States, they have been influenced a lot by white ideas. I was never accepted by an Asian community. The only time I felt accepted was by other Asians . . . my mother's friends who were married to black men or white men or whatever, and their children.

Myra says that her mother told her that she would be considered black to make her strong enough to handle racism. However, Myra has learned a great deal about her Asian heritage, which pleases her mother.

African-American is a term Myra uses, but she says that being American is just as important to her as being black: "There is so much about the African-American culture in itself that we need to discover. I strongly identify myself as an African-American. And I understand that I have African ancestors—but that's exactly what they are."

Myra holds many leadership positions at Whelan, and says that she has experienced racism because she is a minority with leadership positions in majority-white organizations:

I had a white student who was president of a student organization say that he didn't feel that a minority-led organization could ever truly represent, could ever truly lead, the student body because that person didn't represent the majority of students. What he was saying to me is that because I am a minority, and I was running the organization I just wasn't good enough because really there should have been a white person. . . . To have someone be that bold to say that two feet away from me and feel that comfortable—you know, I went off.

Myra has never experienced virulent racism, but she believes that it is difficult to call most incidents that happen racist:

The thing about racism today, and my peers will agree with me, it is not so overt that you can say this was an incident of racism. My brother was stopped by [a] police officer saying he could be in a stolen vehicle. I perceive that as racist, because all he had to do is look up the license plate to find out, or car type or whatever. He gave my brother no justification besides you might be driving a stolen vehicle. He didn't call my brother any names. He didn't make race an issue.

Conservatives, in Myra's view, believe that African-Americans should be self-sufficient and are nonsupportive of welfare and affirmative action. Moderates are liberal when it comes to economics, but more conservative on social issues. They have more of a mixture of conservative and liberal views. Liberals believe in more government control and regulatory policies. They also "look out for minority constituents." She would call her father a moderate and her mother a liberal. She considers herself a moderate, saying that she "reflects her father's views."

Myra believes that all the problems of poverty, drugs, and crime in the black community are due to the number of single-parent households in the black community:

> It's a cycle. It's a [recurring] process. You have a mother who is a single parent. She might have been a young mother. She's heavily reliant on the public education system. The children go there, and they don't receive the type of attention and care that they need. I have personal examples of going into public schools that serve predominantly low-income and predominantly African-American communities, where teachers just sit and stare at their children and don't even teach; where students are put in learning disability centers and not even touched to see if they really have a learning disability. Young girls who are left alone at home, who don't have any strong male presence—it's happening over and over again—and you have a young mother.

Myra says these problems can be solved by the efforts of African-Americans who have been successful, if they worked to change these communities: "We have so many African-Americans that are coming out of Ivy League schools. To me it just seems ridiculous that our communities could be in this state. If everybody used their education, their economics to help lift those in the lower brackets I don't think there would ever be a problem."

Myra supports affirmative action, and completes the sentence "In the United States, if black people don't do well in life, it is because . . . "

with "social environment." She also supports welfare reform, and spending on crime prevention rather than punishment. Myra is liberal on abortion, premarital sex, and having children out-of-wedlock, but is less than neutral on tolerance of homosexuality.

Myra has voted twice in elections and is an Independent. She voted for Clinton in the 1992 election because she was attracted to his "campaign style." She admires Harvey Gantt, the former mayor of Charlotte, North Carolina, who challenged Jesse Helms for his senate seat and lost. Myra knows that Louis Farrakhan "has a lot of power," but is not aware of anything he has done for the black community. Regarding the Nation of Islam, she has "never understood what that organization is all about."

While espousing liberal views on many issues, Myra Mason places the blame for problems in the black community on the "social environment," and expects those problems to be solved by middle class members of the black community. She does not blame racism for the problems, nor does she expect government to solve the problems. She has opted to learn about her Asian ancestry, but makes it clear that she identifies herself as a black person because that is how others perceive her. Her multicultural identity has been sublimated by the reality of her treatment by others, as well as by her mother, who felt the need to prepare her children for life in the United States. The current effort of persons with multiracial backgrounds to have classifications that acknowledge both parents is frustrating to some African-Americans who may feel that they are thereby denying their black racial group membership. Others feel that this also denies what some think of as an absolute truth—that even partial African-American group membership means bona fide group membership, and subjection to all of the attending stereotypes by the outside world.

Summary

These politically moderate students indicate that linkages between racial group membership and life experiences are difficult to make in the absence of parental instruction or enlightenment on the subject.

For example, Marilyn Lacey indicated that her mother was apolitical, and never discussed or expressed views on racial issues. Morgan Stone, on the other hand, has been told many stories of his father's experiences. This has helped shape his strong racial group identity.

If parents leave politics out of the body of wisdom they pass on to their children, there is ample room for influence by the leadership of the day. Unfortunately, many of the students were hard-pressed to come up with any names of influential political leaders in the black community, local or national. Marie Potter, Marilyn Lacey, and Matthew Williams all responded that they could think of no influential black political leaders. Morgan Stone named Cornel West, who is a legitimate choice but not an elected official.

Morris, Hatchett, and Brown write that "political socialization is not a process with a beginning or end but one occurring within and shaped by historical context" (Morris, Hatchett, and Brown 1988:300). The context in which these students came of age was one in which racism was declared to have been conquered, and complaints of discrimination were derided as "excuses." The effects of this kind of atmosphere are seen in the manner in which these young people respond to questions regarding their experiences with racism. While all reported such experiences, they also exhibited a tendency to diminish their effects or consequences. Sometimes they were extremely reticent to even name such incidents as racist. This sublimation of emotional awareness of race in their lives may be a factor in the development of more moderate attitudes. In the next chapter, liberal students with an acute awareness of racial issues reveal how socioeconomic status, experiences with racism, and environment helped to shape their political views.

5

Identity and Integration
The Liberals

The young black Republicans whose views we have examined so far believe that problems in the African-American community are not entirely the fault of whites. They also believe that even if whites are responsible in part, they cannot solve those problems. These young men are attracted to the Republican Party because of the self-help ideas of the Jack Kemp variety. Another appealing feature of the Republican Party platform is its stance on moral and cultural issues. The strong racial group identity of the Republican race men has resulted in a hybrid of traditional conservatism and nationalism.

The black students at majority-white institutions, who comprise most of the students in this chapter, illustrate the developmental path that identity and ideology may take when blacks are in the minority and solidarity is both personally rewarding and beneficial in the competition for university resources. There are nine students featured in this chapter. Six are from single-parent households, two are attending historically black institutions, and only one is from a solidly middle class background.

Resolving to Be Radical

Lawrence Sims—Woodson University

Lawrence Sims was born and raised in a large northeastern city, and projects a quiet intensity throughout the interview. He attended preparatory school from the ages of fourteen to seventeen, and was raised in a single-parent home. Lawrence has a strained relationship with both parents, but seems close to his grandmother. Active in a black fraternity and other organizations on campus, Lawrence refers to race constantly. When asked about the Catholic, predominantly white elementary school he attended, he replies that it constituted his "first dealings and encounters with institutionalized racism and a white patriarchal society." Lawrence's most bitter memory is the corporal punishment meted out by the sisters:

> I remember having a hard time dealing with being beat by these women. They had what they called the board of education, which was a paddle that they would—I'll never forget it because it really annoyed me that these women—part of it was just being a rebellious youngster, but even that these women were not my mother and particularly white women doing this to me. I had a hard time dealing with that.

He was failed in the third grade, although, according to him, he was not a poor student. Lawrence feels the teachers did not understand him and underestimated his ability. When he left for an all-black elementary school, he became an honor student. His junior high school was also all-black, and Lawrence believed that because the principal and assistant principal were nurturing and supportive black women, students were inspired to perform.

Lawrence was able to participate in a program for minority students that allowed him to attend a preparatory school away from home. It was here that he first became aware of his status as a black person—at least in the eyes of his white classmates. In one incident, a black classmate got the better of a white classmate in a heated debate. When the black student walked away from the class, Lawrence says that the white student commented, "What's her problem? She must not realize my father pays her tuition."

Lawrence was taken aback by the comment, a testament to what he feels was his naiveté regarding the importance of race. According to Lawrence, this naiveté led him to befriend too many white people too quickly. He says that he looks back at pictures of himself in preparatory school and during his first year at Woodson and sees a person trying too hard to fit in and doing "silly" things. When he became involved in the Black Student Alliance during his sophomore and junior years, he became less concerned about fitting in with whites, and his black identity grew stronger.

Lawrence no longer has white friends because as he became more aware of racial issues, it was harder to maintain relationships with whites. In part it was because of their denial of the privilege that he believes being white brings. The acceptance of this privilege and power, for Lawrence, is tantamount to condoning racism. He mentions the lynching of Emmett Till, the Tuskegee Experiments, and Cointelpro as examples of why he finds it difficult to trust whites.[1] Sometimes just being in the classroom with whites, observing their attitudes, and hearing their opinions on things affects him negatively.

He tells a story that illustrates why he finds it so difficult to trust whites. Once when returning to boarding school, he was forced to leave the train after having words with the conductor. The police were summoned and he was asked to leave. When he finally arrived at school, the Dean assumed the incident was his fault. Although some of his classmates had witnessed the run-in, which Lawrence believes was a result of racism on the part of the conductor, none spoke up for him.

Although Lawrence is aware that he has had opportunities that many other young men of his background have not had, he still believes that blacks are connected with each other through "a collective struggle and a collective experience. There are different struggles for different blacks, but it is the same because we all look the same. A collective history." He also thinks that families and regional ties are strong enough to create important intraracial differences; therefore the strongest link, in Lawrence's view, is the shared history of slavery and oppression.

This link could be strengthened by increased knowledge of black history. Lawrence believes that once they review this history, blacks will realize that the white man is responsible for much of what ails the black community. He says that "Everything we've contributed has been taken away from us. . . . We are responsible for each other. We are responsible for our brothers and sisters."

This idea of responsibility for one another is one of the hallmarks of liberal ideology. Lawrence does not hesitate to define himself as a liberal. He makes it clear that he is talking about a white conservative when he says that he or she is "someone who feels or believes in individual responsibility. They believe that everyone starts out the same and refuse to recognize the mechanisms that keep a people oppressed." He adds that conservatives do not understand how difficult it is to get out of poor black neighborhoods and "make something of your life." He comments that black conservatives such as Clarence Thomas know how difficult life is for poor blacks, which makes their conservatism feel more like betrayal.

Lawrence Sims is militant in his view of where problems of crime and drugs in the black community originate and why they are so difficult to solve:

> [The] white man's God complex. The belief that the white man is inherently more intelligent and better than blacks because it has created an inferiority complex in the black community. It's an embedded mind-set that we can't be president—it has created a negative mechanism that is ongoing. We have been forced to deal with so many internal divisions based on gender, based on complexion, and just on and on—that has divided us in so many different ways.

While Lawrence does not balk at blaming racism for black problems, he is more of a traditional liberal on abortion, homosexuality, and premarital sex. However, when it comes to having children outside the marital bond, he moves definitively to the right in expressing his disapproval. He explains that his views come from his own experience: "It's something that I think is done best in a marriage, particularly a healthy marriage, a healthy bond. My mother had me and my siblings out of wedlock, and it creates many problems." Lawrence believes that his "psyche has been distorted," and his relationship with his father is ill-defined.

Although he says that society is sexist, and thinks that women have not achieved equality, Lawrence also believes that sexism is different for black women than for white women:

> Sexism creates problems in black households. Black women's salaries are higher than men['s] because of affirmative action. Black women

are a "two-fer"—a black and a woman. The practice of hiring black women over men is corrupt, racist, and sexist. It creates a communication gap between black men and women.

Lawrence cannot offer any proof that black women are being hired in greater numbers than black men, but the perception that black women are taking jobs away from black men is clearly implied in his statement.

Lawrence has a political ideology deeply rooted in the black nationalist philosophy of Malcolm X. Lawrence names Louis Farrakhan, Ben Chavis, Malcolm X, and Marcus Garvey as some of the people who have influenced his views. His strong racial group identity and his political attitudes were forged from his beginnings in all-black environments. They were clearly reinforced by his integration experience both at the boarding school and at Woodson. He believes that Woodson does not welcome black students, and he does not feel a part of the student body. Evidence of Woodson's less than welcoming environment is its failure to hire enough blacks to serve on the faculty. When they are hired, Lawrence says that "[they are] extremely bogged down with their own responsibilities . . . being put on ad hoc committees and trying to gain tenureship." Lawrence expresses concern about the dual appointments of many of the black professors. He feels appointments in two departments mean that they have twice as much to do. Lawrence says he has no white friends, and he spends his time working to change the atmosphere for African-American students at Woodson.

Lawrence Sims faced real challenges in resolving conflict about his racial group identity. He was helped in resolving his identity crisis by courses on black history and politics. Reassessing his experiences in light of this new knowledge, Lawrence emerged with a liberal ideology that put the blame for black problems on oppression by whites.

Barriers to Racial Integration and Racial Solidarity

Liz Thompson—Woodson University

The next student, Liz Thompson, relates her growing sense of the importance of racial group identity to being placed in a majority-white environment. Unlike Lawrence, who experienced a crisis of identity in high school and spent his college years redefining himself, this young woman resolved identity issues in high school. This was when Liz became aware of the importance of racial identity, which has become more acute since her arrival at Woodson. Her high school was a "magnet" school established for academically gifted students. Only a few blacks attended, and Liz found that the student body divided itself along ethnic lines. When she observed that European and Latino ethnic groups segregated themselves from whites, it seemed natural to her that African-Americans would too, especially since blacks felt especially alienated.

Liz Thompson is from the same northeastern city as Lawrence, and is the daughter of a West Indian mother. She has not led a privileged life, but her mother has worked hard to provide her with the best formal education, as well as personally enriching educational experiences. She has traveled out of the country extensively with her mother, and comments that these trips have been invaluable to her.

When asked if there is a black identity, Liz is unsure about how to determine whether someone has a black identity or not: "There are students here, black students, that don't hang out with black people and they join white Greek organizations—and to me they don't fit the black identity. But I'm not really sure that is the way to judge." Liz does feel that all blacks are linked: "We are all family even though we are spread all across the earth. I just feel that there is a link somewhere inside." She also thinks that blacks at Woodson are more connected than students at historically black colleges. As an example of this connection she cites the unspoken rule that all blacks on campus must acknowledge each other when they meet, whether they know each other or not. Liz says that she does not believe students at black colleges have this rule. She had the same experience in her magnet high school. Liz says they "pulled themselves together" even if they did not like each other—"just for the sake of being together." Whites were separated along ethnic lines as well.

Attending school at Woodson makes Liz aware of stereotypes about blacks, and she tells an amusing story about how this fear of being stereotyped affects her:

Just the other day in the University Center they had four hours of jazz playing and they had wings [buffalo wings], and so forth. AT&T came to try to do business on the campus and they were giving away things. And if you filled out a survey in another eating area they gave away basketballs. So anyway, as I was leaving, I was running out trying to get the shuttle and I had a basketball in one hand and a chicken wing in the other hand. And I was running and I was thinking, "Boy, I must really look like what they think all black people are."

When asked about her experiences with racism, she relates the story of a high school counselor who prevented her from applying to majority-white four-year colleges and universities by refusing to release her transcript except to community colleges and historically black colleges:

> And so my mother went and spoke to him and he told my mother he was sorry but that most of the black students just went to black schools, so he didn't know what to tell me. And so my mother asked him, well, where do you send your Asian students? We found out he [had] told previous black students the same thing.

Liz's mother obtained a copy of the transcript in an unorthodox way, and sent it to several four-year colleges on her own. Liz notes that without an assertive mother, she would have been relegated to attending a community college. She laments the fact that many other black students may have been denied opportunities by accepting this counselor's actions.

Another experience that has affected Liz was related by a friend who visited relatives in Alabama. The Ku Klux Klan stopped him and a few friends in a car on a deserted road. They did not hurt them physically but made them strip and lie on the ground. They succeeded in badly frightening him, leaving him somewhat traumatized. She says this incident "sticks in her mind" because it happened not long ago and it left her friend damaged.

These experiences make it difficult for Liz to forge friendships with whites. She says she has two white friends, but then qualifies that by saying:

> But I only let them get to a certain point—then it stops. And a lot of times I don't do it consciously but when I look back at it I say, well,

how come I'm not as close with the white people as I am with the black people? And I think a lot of times it's just because on this campus there are so many different things happening. Like I said before I don't think a lot of white people can understand what's happening with minorities. And so, rather than me just come out and tell them, well, this is what's wrong and wait for them to agree—I just don't say anything.

When asked how she limits the growth of her relationships with white students, Liz says that she does not go on outings with them to the movies or restaurants. They do visit each other's dorm rooms, but they rarely get past the acquaintance level. Her black friendships, she notes, do not require that things be said—they are simply understood. In other words, Liz has developed no primary relationships with white students, only secondary ones.

Raised in a household with her grandmother and mother, Liz says her grandmother is ideologically conservative and her mother is moderate to conservative. She, however, is liberal. When asked how she defines "conservative," Liz immediately thinks of a *black* conservative when she hears the term:

I don't like it. There is a certain type of person I think of when I hear that word conservative. I think of the black person who is conservative who says we don't need welfare and that the government is not at fault for anything that happens to minorities. And I just don't like it.

Liz believes that white conservatives are given more credibility when blacks agree with their ideas. When she thinks of a white conservative, it does not inspire a reaction in her. She ignores white conservatives. Liberals accept anything as long as it doesn't impose on anyone else's freedom. Moderates, in her view, are more fair. They can "go from one side to the other depending on the situation."

Her views are liberal on most issues with the exception of premarital sex, of which she disapproves because of her religious convictions. However, like many of the other students in this survey, she is ambivalent about affirmative action. Liz and her friends support affirmative action, but she says that "none of us wants to be in a situation where we are the token person." She believes companies would not hire blacks without affirmative action, and that it will be needed for some years to come.

She blames problems of poverty, drugs, and crime in the black community on a lack of education, and believes more black role models are needed for children in poor communities. In her view, government has a responsibility to guarantee racial equality by supporting affirmative action and improving public schools. Liz sees many problems in the welfare system, but believes it should be restructured and more money spent, not less. She is less concerned about the Republican "Contract with America" and how it will affect blacks.

Liz Thompson was integrated with whites at an early age, and her experiences have resulted in intensifying her feelings of separation from white society. She was exposed to whites in school; however, her neighborhood was all-black, as were her associations outside school. Liz, her mother, and her grandmother attend a large African Methodist Episcopal (AME) church, and she participates in church activities. Her home life has helped her forge a strong sense of racial group identity, and because she has never established close friendships with whites, her black identity remains primary.

Lawrence Sims and Liz Thompson both illustrate how the ideal of integration has been obstructed by the exclusion of blacks from white peer groups, by blacks' perception that whites cannot or will not understand their experiences as blacks, and by encounters with racism in their own lives as well as the lives of friends and family. Lawrence and Liz are both sensitive regarding affirmative action, and both have been profoundly affected by their experiences in majority-white situations.

A Liberal Nationalist with a Feminist Flair

Lana Tolliver—Woodson University

Lana Tolliver is a dancer, writer, and organizer of volunteer services at Woodson University. She auditioned for a place in a summer workshop with a well-known New York dance company, and was chosen for a slot. Lana is from a single-parent home and is the oldest of five children. Born and raised in the southern city in which Woodson is located, Lana says she first became aware of her race and its significance when she attended the performing arts high school in the city. She was cognizant of economic differences between the races at a very early age: "When I was smaller, I knew there was a difference between blacks and whites, but I thought it was that whites had money, and blacks didn't. [Laughs] Although I wasn't very far off." Lana lived in an all-black neighborhood and attended all-black schools before being admitted to the majority-white performing arts school.

She definitely feels connected to other blacks, and says that it is because of "threads of commonality" that run through the race. Lana feels that all blacks struggle against "the stereotypes that have been placed on you since America even existed." All blacks share the way they are viewed by whites. Black identity, in Lana's view, means that you feel connected to Africa, and you are "conscious of the subjugation of your people and the richness of your ancestry."

Lana believes Louis Farrakhan is wonderful, and says that his emphasis on black solidarity is what disturbs whites. When asked if she is a separatist, she answers affirmatively. When asked why she chose to attend Woodson if she believes that African-Americans are better off separated from whites, she responds: "I'm a separatist but I don't think that—I think that we could live with other people as long as we know who we are." She says Utopia to her would be a society in which blacks lived, worked, and conducted business separately from whites. Blacks would have total control of their own community and could restrict whites' access to the community.

Lana was influenced ideologically by a high school friend who practiced Islam. She says that the relationship "started me to question everything I was doing. . . . I didn't know a lot of people that I know now as far as Huey Newton and Angela Davis—these were not household names in my family." The Rodney King beating deeply affected Lana. She was a senior in high school when the incident occurred, and says:

I was completely—to me it was a slap in the face. It was like racism . . . they blatantly showed racism in this country. Blatantly . . . they didn't even try to pacify us by condemning these people. They didn't even wear the mask. And to me that said something about the direction that black people were headed in this country.

Lana tried to talk to one of her favorite white teachers about her anger and frustration over the Rodney King incident, but found the teacher remote and unable to empathize with her feelings. The encounter changed her feelings about the teacher, and she now thinks that it is impossible for whites to understand a black perspective on issues of race.

She has had an experience at Woodson that she thinks was due to racism on the part of an English professor. In her freshman year, Lana went to see this professor about a "C" on an essay. She says that the professor told her that blacks were known for their inability to write, and that her "C" was to be expected. When asked how she responded, she answered:

I responded by becoming associate editor of the newsletter here and majoring in English. I remember saying, "You've got to be kidding. You mean to say that Maya Angelou as an African-American can't write, or she couldn't write—or Angela Davis—all these profound writers. They shouldn't be where they are according to your theory." The professor said that they had to learn it. He said that he wasn't saying blacks couldn't learn, but they had to be trained.

For Lana, there is no doubt that whites in general perceive that blacks are less capable, and are unwilling and unable to treat blacks equitably.

In answering questions about problems she perceives in the black community, Lana focuses on the addictions. She believes drugs are deliberately placed in the black community by those in power: "These depressants are chemical depressants that are contributing to our present condition." The answer for Lana is black control of businesses that locate in the black community. She says blacks need to say "No, you can't move here." If the number of retail liquor stores were diminished and the community cleaned up, Lana feels that many of the problems would disappear. She feels that the addicts cannot reason or work their way out of conditions of poverty, and those who are not addicted are too busy working and dealing with their own problems to help the addicts.

Lana and her friends talk a lot about the double bind of racism and sexism. Lana mentions how the rape charges against the boxer Mike Tyson affected her:

> This was a black man and a black woman. You're caught in between whether or not this black man violated this black woman in the most extreme and horrendous way ever. And then you're caught between this black man. He got up in society. He has a vision. And every time—you've got to watch yourself if you're a black man and you're making too much money. They don't like it. Something's going to happen where all of it is taken away. You're being punished. And they [black women] have that side where you want to be an abolitionist for that person. . . .

Lana's desire to defend black men who she thinks are under attack by a racist legal system is strong. She says she is struggling with reconciling her concerns about race issues and the status of black women within the race, especially since she became aware of stumbling blocks placed in her mother's career path. The O. J. Simpson trial sparked conversations between Lana and her friends about interracial relationships: "Now, when I say we talk about interracial relationships we really don't care too much about the person—the white women these males are with. To me, we just basically conclude that they have particular insecurities—these black men."

Lana describes herself as a liberal, and says all her friends are "militant black women." She thinks conservatives are primarily concerned with conformity:

> When I think of conservative I think of suits, anal retention. [Laughs] No, I think of someone who conforms to what society standardizes at what you're supposed to be. Not open or willing to accept anything that diverges or differs from that societal standard. And I think that conservative is male-oriented, usually. And white male-oriented. And anything outside the boundaries of what the white male-oriented deems . . . you're supposed to be is not conservative. But if you fall into that, or conform to those norms—that's conservative to me.

A liberal for Lana is "Myself. One who does not allow someone else to dictate their actions, even if it does not conform to societal norms." Moderates, in Lana's view, are those who conform to the norm when they believe it to be appropriate. They are not completely closed, however, to expressing themselves outside these norms.

Lana's political views are aligned with her liberal ideological perspective and her strong sense of racial group identity. She sees affirmative action as necessary, and views the current criticism of the practice as proof that blacks are "regressing." Lana believes the government is responsible for ensuring racial equality. Her idea is to spend less on defense and more on education and creating jobs. Welfare should be reformed to place more emphasis on work, but more money should be spent, not less. Lana says that the rich should be taxed to pay for job training. She is liberal on abortion and most other moral and cultural issues with the exception of homosexuality, on which she is moderate. She voted for Clinton in the 1992 election, and encouraged her friends to vote.

Lana Tolliver grew up in an environment that was tough to negotiate, and offered little in the way of resources. She identifies with those who remain in that environment, and she gears her volunteer efforts toward helping young people in the inner city. Attending a majority-white high school and Woodson University have resulted in experiences that have solidified Lana's sense that African-Americans are systematically oppressed by white society.

The Triple Bind of Race, Gender, and Class

Lynn Stevens—Windsor University

A native southerner, Lynn Stevens is a petite and lively student with a crown of dreadlocks. Lynn's formidable intellect is evident in her countenance and the way she expresses herself. Lynn chose to attend Windsor, a predominantly white university, because she believed it to be the best university in her home state. She is from an impoverished family and is eligible for a sizable amount of financial aid because she is an in-state student. Being at Windsor "is a learning experience," Lynn says with a laugh. She has been surprised at the number of black middle-class professionals in the town surrounding Windsor. She feels that she has struggled socially at Windsor. This has been more difficult for her than the academic struggles she has encountered. Lynn says:

> Well, I think I came in very naive and very idealistic. And I thought that the black people would be like me. Sort of like from a working-class family—had, you know, single mother. I didn't count on meeting, like a bourgeois, sort of like upper-middle-class blacks who necessarily didn't like me. You know, they wouldn't like me because of my hair or because I thought that black people here, especially at a predominantly white school—I thought it would be more united, more cohesive. That was a shock, I was disappointed. Trying to get involved in the Black Student Alliance was hard because if you weren't in a Greek, if you weren't a member of the Greek organization that the president happened to be a member of, you didn't, it was hard for you to get on committees.

Lynn finds the black Greeks petty and shallow at Windsor. She would not join a sorority for this reason, but notes that she would be unable to join anyway because of the money required. Lynn says that another thing that separates her from the black middle-class students is her hairstyle. Her dreadlocks are in the early stages, and students perceive this style to mean that she is politically radical. Most black women on the Windsor campus wear their hair in straight styles that require a chemical relaxer.

Lynn is distressed at gender issues between black men and women on campus. Black women, she says, seem desperate to gain the attention of black men on campus:

> I think, it's sort of sad but I respect myself. And a lot of black women here don't respect themselves. Or they say they respect themselves but like, they'll take things from the black men here, or they'll chase after black men. Even freshmen are all caught up in the hoopla. Oh, Windsor, Windsor men, black intelligent men—and even when I was all caught up in that like I was say, you know, whatever—I'm not taking

this, and I would like, you know, leave people alone. Leave these guys alone. Guys would tell me that I was too serious and too intense.

She just realized during the week of the interview that she is a feminist. In the past, Lynn had associated feminism exclusively with white women. She has learned through a study of black feminist literature that while black feminists may have a different agenda than white women, they are still feminists:

> Black feminists are for the development of the black community as a whole . . . like for the affirmation of black women but for the uplifting of the black man, therefore sitting down and discussing issues and problems in the community and trying to settle them. That's along the line of "womanist." I think Alice Walker came up with that term.

Lynn and her friends have discussed this topic a lot lately because of a recent controversy surrounding the Women's Center on campus:

> The committee [at the Center] that brings programming for black or women of color to campus, they separated from the Women's Center. They felt like the Women's Center wasn't being supportive of women of color issues. They were focusing on white feminist issues. It is typical of white women, or white people in general, to feel like their agenda is everyone's agenda. That they can speak for everyone. They just assume . . . I guess they think the world gravitates around them. That's my own personal opinion. I support it [the separation]. I feel like it's a statement.

Lynn moved frequently while growing up, but spent most of her formative years in public housing. The environment was very oppressive:

> Our project was really bad. If someone needed an ambulance, the ambulance would wait at the bottom of the bridge and you [had] to get your way down there some kind of way. They weren't going to go up. Violent. Something was always happening.

In junior high and high school Lynn felt awkward because she was placed in accelerated all-white classes. Some of her classmates knew little about black people and often insulted her. Although she became fairly comfortable in these classes over time, Lynn did not feel accepted by the black students outside of her classes or the white students in her classes:

> Black students started saying "you're trying to be white." It got to me in the tenth grade. During lunch I would eat with white kids in my class. I started out doing that, but then I stopped and I would just go to the library and eat lunch there and read. It was too awkward, too tense, I felt, to sit and eat lunch with them when all the black kids were on one side.

Lynn was an excellent student in high school, but is disappointed with her academic performance at Windsor. It is clear that the racial stereotype of blacks as incapable of excelling in the sciences has affected her:

> I try really hard. But, I don't know. I was pre-med up until last semester, so I was average—like a "C." I'm still trying to come to terms with that. Now I'm a psychology major and a B or a B+ student, which I'm told isn't competitive enough for graduate school, which distresses me also.

When asked why she is no longer an "A" student, Lynn replies that perhaps it is related to her attempt to major in the "hard" sciences:

> I do well in like my social science classes. So I'm working outside of my strength.
>
> *Why do you persist in working outside of your strength?*
>
> I refuse to, I feel like it shouldn't be that I can't build another strength.... I guess there's a stigma. Black people tend to go into literature or social science. There aren't that many black people in health science, or psychology even. That's not the main reason why I want to go but I would hate to think, um, I'm black and I'm utilizing my language skills. Whether it's because I'm black or just because of my culture that I have strong language skills— or whatever they attribute it to.

Lynn takes it for granted that blacks are more facile with language than science, which indicates how vulnerable black students can be to accepting stereotypical assessments of their abilities in majority-white institutions.

Lynn's "encounter" moment, her first realization that race was meaningful, occurred when she was invited to spend the night with a white family that lived in the housing project: "The kids were like fighting over who I would sleep with. They were like tugging on me. In retrospect, I felt like this baby doll." Other black children in her neighborhood and elementary school also cued Lynn to the fact that being black was not considered a positive thing:

> Black kids and people in my neighborhood would say "you black so-and-so"—name-calling. It really hurt my feelings. I don't know—I was just very sensitive. I became very conscious of how dark I was. I felt that everyone thought I was ugly—whites and blacks.
>
> *Do you feel that this kind of prejudice within our own community has diminished?*
>
> I feel like as people grow older, they stop emphasizing it. It's still there. My cousin, he's my age, he goes to Benedict. He only dates light-skinned women. He only finds light-skinned women attractive. He even told me, "Sorry, I have to have a light-skinned woman."

Although Lynn says she is over the pain of being considered unattractive because of her complexion, she admits that it haunts her when she visits the communities in which she volunteers:

> When I work with kids, when I go back into the community, it like hits me. Like I'm going back to where I came from and it's still there. These kids still hate themselves. They call this girl "black" and "nappy-headed." They even come at me and ask "Why do you do your hair like that? Your hair is nappy." It was good for me to say "this is good; this is beautiful; this is natural." They were looking at me like I was crazy. There were white people there, too. I was like, "What's pretty to you?" And they pointed to this blond-headed girl. And I was like, yeah, that's pretty for her, but why isn't what you have pretty?

Carol Changa, profiled in chapter 3, experienced pain as an upper-class woman whose dark skin, in her view, belied her social status. Lynn has experienced pain as a dark-skinned woman whose skin color, in other people's minds, confirms her social status. One study showed that people assign stereotypically black names such as Lakeisha or Sheronda to dark-skinned women, and more European names such as Diane and Laura to light-skinned women, which is a subtle indication of class. In another study, dark-skinned black women are rated by both blacks and whites as being less intelligent and less physically attractive than lighter-skinned black women (Russell, Wilson, and Hall 1992).

Lynn's experience with the term "black" and its loaded meaning early in her life may explain why she prefers it to African-American or any other name:

> I like how, I guess how it was like, brought into existence I guess. Just from what I can remember—civil rights leaders —people in general in the sixties were tired of Negro, colored. They wanted something that was proactive, definitive. I guess like forceful, but assertive—it has power to it, and it's still positive. It's like giving something negative a positive connotation.

Lynn defines a black identity as "being in touch with how my race has been treated historically—and how, um, socially, psychologically, from slavery up until now. Like the effect of different events on us as a race, as a people. African, there's a link to Africa."

Lynn thinks about being black a lot, and thinks that what happens to other blacks will affect her, but it is difficult for her to imagine some day being in a different class from her family:

> It's hard because I'm like in transition, from like working—eventually—class to middle class. And even then, even if I won't be working class like five years from now, it will still affect me just because of my Mom, my brother, and my cousin.

Experiences with racism, for Lynn, have been intense and numerous. She was hard-pressed deciding which ones to relate during the interview. After a long silence, Lynn finally said that she was trying to decide which might be the worst cases:

> I think it's hard because at home the stuff was blatant. Either some redneck would lean out of a truck [and yell] "you nigger" or that kind of thing. But here at Windsor it is very subtle. It has

always been implied, which makes it very frustrating. I feel like I have learned the most from this [subtle racism] than from like blatant name-calling or teachers saying not nice things.

Give me an example of subtle racism.

My freshman year in my dorm—white women who haven't been around black people would skirt around you in the bathroom. They'll look at your hair like "What in the world? What are you doing to your hair?" On the buses, the bus can be packed, and there can be an empty seat beside you and the aisles will be packed and no one will sit in that empty seat beside you. I've had lab TAs [teaching assistants], and I think part of this has to do with the fact that I'm a woman also, but they will single me out and give me special attention. [They will] come over and actually take things from me and try to do my part for my lab for me. That happened to me twice, and I had to go off. It really aggravated me.

Lynn considers herself a liberal. She defines a liberal as someone who is anti-big business, pro-environment, and pro-social programming. Conservatives are usually white males who are Republican and pro-life. Moderates are people who are pro-choice but who would not choose abortion for themselves. Lynn says moderates are not quick to employ racial generalizations and can be sympathetic to black causes.

Lynn believes that poor blacks are victims of a poor public education system. Educational tracking, a system that steers students to either a vocational or a college-preparatory curriculum according to ability, is one aspect of the system that is harmful to black students. Her perspective is balanced by her belief that young blacks are unable to see the value of education, and may not be trying as hard as they should to obtain one. Lynn believes that one of the best strategies for eliminating the problems in the system are black middle-class role models—not just in schools for a few hours—but living and working in poor black communities. Money would also help alleviate the problems—funding for defense could be reduced to increase funding for education, especially teachers' salaries.

Lynn supports affirmative action and believes welfare reform is headed in the wrong direction—increased funding is needed, not cutbacks. She supports increased funding for the rehabilitation of criminal offenders, but not for prisons. When asked to complete the statement on why black people may not succeed in the United States, Lynn says, "Even if they are qualified for whatever position they're in, they are working in an environment that's not, that is very different from their culture. It wasn't built for them. It is more suited for the white middle-class type." Failure may also be blamed on "internalized oppression."

Lynn is a registered Democrat but says she "votes for whoever is the right person." She voted for Clinton in 1992 because "he wasn't Bush." The only African-American politician Lynn admires is Lenora Fulani, a presidential candidate in the 1988 and 1992 presidential elections.[2] She does not think anyone qualifies as an outstanding leader in a political or social sense. Farrakhan "panders to ignorance," and she is disillusioned about Jesse Jackson:

> I don't like Jesse. I think he is full of rhetoric. It's funny because a friend said he may be doing that to stay alive, 'cause every other black leader who's actually tried to make change has died. I'm disappointed that he has not made change. He's just talking. I also feel like he's looking out for the interests of the upper-middle class.
>
> *Where do you think you got that idea?*
>
> I don't see him in the community. He's like in Washington. Also Joe Clark came to speak, and a lot of the things he said about Jesse made sense, just about how the African-American thing . . . he said Jesse coined that, like brought that back. He felt like it was something to revive the black middle class. To me it's a superficial way to revive people. I just like action, change, tangible change.

Lynn Stevens, a witness to the cruelest of southern perversions and predilections, struggles to find her way in a world where caste and complexion influence how she is accepted by both blacks and whites. Another young woman a few years ahead of Lynn at Windsor, who does not share her socioeconomic background or her complexion, nevertheless reveals a similar struggle to reconcile issues of race and class as she negotiates her way through Windsor.

Leah Somers—Windsor University

Leah Somers is a soft-spoken young woman who states immediately that she is unhappy at Windsor and feels very isolated. She is from the Midwest, and her mother is her sole supporter. After attending a summer program at Windsor and being thoroughly impressed with the prestige enjoyed by students at the university, she decided to attend. Leah now thinks she made a mistake:

> The social atmosphere is not really one that, it doesn't really fit me. Nor does the political atmosphere. I think I would have been much better off in an environment that was not so stringent, or difficult academically as well. I'm not saying that I would have taken the easy way but then I would have had more confidence to excel in more things. To come into a different environment and be bombarded with all of these difficult things to handle at one time tends to work on one's self-esteem. Also not to be surrounded by black people, people that I have something in common with. It was a very difficult transition that I didn't realize until this year.
>
> *What did you think was happening at first?*
>
> I just thought, well, I read in psychology about this theory that everyone reaches their peak and then they decline. You have a certain amount of potential that you're born with and once you reach it that's it. Then you're burned out. I was like, gosh, my senior year must've been that peak and now I'm just on my way down. I thought I just wasn't good enough. I'm just not good enough. I don't have these thoughts; I don't have these theories that we're supposed to have. I don't have the background we're supposed to have. I have no clue.

Leah sounds much like Lynn when talking about her academic performance, attributing her failure to her own shortcomings. Both wonder whether their academic problems are somehow related to racial or cultural differences. Leah is uncomfortable with the kinds of social activities that are common at universities with vital Greek organizations. This discomfort is connected to her overall feelings of alienation from campus life and frustration at her fellow classmates' failure to acknowledge the community, specifically the black community, that exists all around the campus:

> I guess overall, since it's predominantly white and that's the culture that influences the social activities. And then under that, fraternities, white fraternities, they influence the things there are to do greatly. And a lot of their things are to get together and drink, and party, and I don't do that. And then you have the black culture which is very much separated, both physically and culturally separated from the rest of the Windsor community. The problem there is that a lot of us come from pretty affluent backgrounds. I won't say us. [Laughs] And even if it's not affluent, Windsor is just the kind of place where everything is here and you could go on forever and you could go four years and not leave the campus and not need or want for anything. I think it's too protected. And students who are not even so . . . wealthy are still in that protected environment. And I think we've lost sight as black people of where our struggle is and what's going on with other people who are not at Windsor.

Student awareness of the plight of black people, both in the surrounding community and the country at large, is important to Leah. Underneath her distress and discomfort at Windsor is the fear that blacks there have forgotten their connection with less fortunate blacks. When asked to define what black identity is, Leah replies that it is shared oppression:

> I think it's just knowing how other people relate to you because of your skin color. And beyond that there is difference. You don't have to listen to a certain kind of music to be black. You have to know what it's like to be treated as "less than" because of your skin color.

Leah believes that people have to grow into a black identity, because the realization of your subordinate status comes over time. She thinks about being black a lot, and believes her fate is definitely tied to the fate of other blacks.

Leah prefers to be called "black" rather than African-American:

> I love it [the term "black"]. Black is me. African-American to me is saying a couple of things. It's saying, one, that I don't really belong here. That I have some type of hyphenated identity. It belongs to me. Africa belongs to me . . . and I think it's included in "black." And then also, I think there needs to be some kind of distinction for people who are African-American. I'm not African-American.

Leah's first realization of her racial group membership came at an early age—while she was in a majority-white preschool:

> There I was pretty much ignored. The kids would ask me questions that I really didn't understand why or what. All my dolls were white and I wanted to be white. And I had long hair, but I wanted it not to have to be pressed or processed in order for me to straighten it. It was a class thing, too. They automatically assumed I didn't have any money—even though I dressed better than most of them because my mother made sure that even if we didn't have money, I definitely wasn't going to dress worse than anybody.

This experience, combined with family conversations she overheard about race, made her aware that being black had some significance. When she talked about her classmates at home, her grandmother would always inquire about the race of the person. Asked if she had ever experienced racism, Leah first answers no, then changes her mind. She remembers an experience in a class at Windsor in which a group assignment became uncomfortable when she was shut out of group discussions:

> They would sit with me, but they would crowd me out—their backs would be turned. I just sat there at first and I said OK, maybe it's because—I don't know. I couldn't think of anything except that either it's I'm a woman, or I'm black, or it's both. I didn't really know how to approach it or how to say anything.

Leah's professor noticed the behavior of the group and was displeased. He wanted her to do something about it, but assured her that he would take care of it if she was uneasy. She arranged to meet the group leader and discuss the situation. When she asked if he was aware of shutting her out of the group meetings, he said he was not aware that this was happening. He insisted that he was not prejudiced and cited having black friends as evidence of such. Leah says that this was the "first time I realized that prejudice does exist." The experience was all the more frustrating because of the group leader's denial that it happened.

Leah's strong sense of racial group identity and experiences like the one related above may have resulted in the formation of classic liberal attitudes on political issues. Leah associates conservatives with the Republican Party, whites, and the wealthy, and surprisingly, with the Ku Klux Klan. She thinks the primary characteristic of a conservative is that they "do not understand minorities or any type of disadvantaged group." Moderates are "wishy-washy," while liberals are open-minded to radical. Leah believes government has a responsibility to help blacks, and completed the statement "If black people don't do well in life it is because" with "[of] a failure on the part of the government coupled with a failure on their [black people's] part to hold the government accountable." Government should spend more on education and less on prisons to fulfill its responsibility to minorities and the disadvantaged.

Leah supports welfare reform but thinks more money should be spent, not less. On moral and cultural issues she is moderate to liberal, expressing conditional support for abortion and premarital sex, and tolerance for homosexuality and having children out of wedlock. Although she supports women's rights, Leah believes that minority women are not being well represented because "you have that issue of am I black today or am I a woman today? How can I be both? And that's a difficult choice."

A registered Democrat, Leah has voted more than three times. One of the main reasons she voted for Clinton in 1992 was because she felt he might reverse some of the cuts in student aid made during the Reagan-Bush administrations. She also supported Clinton's emphasis on domestic issues over international issues. She names Sharon Pratt-Kelly, former mayor of the District of Columbia, as the only African-American politician she admires. She respects Jesse Jackson for his "presence" in American politics. When asked for her thoughts on Louis Farrakhan, Leah replied:

I think he's entitled to his views, although they are not congruent with mine in every respect. I think he's right on a lot of counts, too, as far as the black community uniting. I think his ideas are sound, it's just his methods . . . the radicalness turns some people away . . . people who would otherwise support him.

Leah feels that the Nation of Islam is gaining credibility in the black community by fulfilling deep needs. However, she is sad that "less radical black institutions, churches being one, cannot compete, and are not meeting that need."

Limited Identity and Liberal Attitudes

Lee Vinson—Windsor University

Lee Vinson, a decidedly apolitical kind of student, is thoughtful and well-spoken. Born and raised in the Southwest, Lee's father was in the military and his mother held a white-collar job. The majority of Lee's high school friends were white. He estimates that today at least ten or fifteen of his good friends are white. He was a good student in high school, and after a rocky first semester at Windsor, maintains more than a 3.0 grade point average.

Lee thinks about being black a lot these days because he is taking a number of courses in which blacks are being discussed. In one course he is studying the Harlem Renaissance, and in another social issues such as welfare and affirmative action. He thinks that what happens generally to other blacks will only affect him some, and defines black identity in general terms:

I think it's a very difficult thing. Just in a general, broad sense I think black identity is an identification of people who come from a common, shared experience in any proportion. If you're mixed, you have some part of a black identity in common traditions, culture, and roots.

Lee cannot remember a particular moment when he became aware of his racial identity. He thinks that his awareness was gradual, and came from reading and watching television. After he became aware of race, he recognized discrimination when he encountered it in the tenth grade. He told the high school counselor that he wanted to sign up for advanced classes because his freshman year had not challenged him academically. She was reluctant, according to Lee, because "she was just assuming that I couldn't do it. And I knew it only had to be on the basis of my color, because nobody else was in the program. No other black person was in advanced English and all those other classes. I just couldn't understand her rationale. I was a good student, so she couldn't have been basing it on my performance." This has been Lee's only personal experience with racism. His friends, however, experienced problems while on Spring Break at Daytona Beach, Florida:

> They came back really frustrated, saying "why can't the white people ever . . . why can't we experience the fun that they had." They would be in a club dancing with a white girl and her friends would come and take her away. There was a black girl there, and she was absolutely beautiful—but she would only dance with white men and she would only talk to white men. I was just like I'm so lucky 'cause I've never had to experience those situations. I've always missed them—like they went to Daytona and I went to Tampa. I think I'm lucky because I don't think I'd be the appropriate person to react in those situations.
>
> *Why?*
>
> I don't want to sound conceited or anything but I'm too intelligent about the situations . . . that have happened. And because of class I've learned how to speak about racism and discrimination in an intellectual mode and I don't think I would ever stop and let things pass. I'll go to the highest level. I'll do whatever I can to get my own justice.

This ability to be articulate is important to Lee, because it enables him to communicate with whites:

> White people in this society run society and you have to be able to talk their language and make them respect you. I think the only way that a lot of white people will respect black people is if they have this degree, or are able to spell this word, or are able to do these different things. I

basically, personally, have an ulterior motive. I may get up there but I'm bringing somebody else with me.

Here Lee expresses a feeling of obligation to other blacks, in spite of his lack of an "encounter" experience and his limited experiences with racism.

Lee defines a political conservative as a white male, but adds that he is "intelligent enough to know that it is bigger than that. It basically means that they are not willing to—they're very tight . . . really strict—morally and economically." Moderates employ common sense when deciding political issues. They won't go to either extreme. Liberals are the opposite of conservatives. They are lenient, rather than strict, in their moral, economic, and political views. Lee is liberal on moral and cultural issues. He supports abortion on demand and is very tolerant of homosexuality.

Although he thinks of himself as only slightly liberal, Lee believes black problems are caused by blacks' exclusion from jobs because of the "good old boy" network, lack of education, and "the vicious cycle of poverty." These problems will be solved by improving education and increasing interaction with middle-class blacks and black college students. He feels that the interaction between black students and workers at Windsor has inspired some to return to school. A woman he speaks with often gives him updates on her progress through one of the local technical schools.

Lee supports affirmative action, and thinks government should in-crease spending on education and decrease spending on defense and foreign aid. He finishes the statement regarding why blacks may not do well in life with "they haven't been given ample opportunities." The main role of government in guaranteeing racial equality, in Lee's view, should be as a strict enforcer of antidiscrimination laws.

Affirmative action had been the topic of discussion in his sociology class:

> We've learned that black is a color, you can't ever fade in or fade out. Those things are always going to be prevalent in people's minds. And the only way for the black community to rise to the level of other communities or receive parity with other ones is through affirmative action.

In a sociology class on welfare Lee has learned to think about the program in a new way:

> It has made me look at a lot of the large ramifications of things that cause people to be in the conditions that they are in. And so that's like, when I think of like, you know, welfare and whatever and giving people money or something. It's not like you're just giving them money but you have to consider everything that they've had to go through and kept them in these positions and placed them there in the first place.

He has only recently learned of the existence of the Nation of Islam and Louis Farrakhan. He heard excerpts from a speech in which Farrakhan made negative remarks about Jewish-Americans: "If someone said the same things about our race on such a large scale I think we would be outraged. I think we should be equally outraged when it happens to someone else." Clearly Lee has led a somewhat sheltered life, having only recently heard of Louis Farrakhan. He believes that black problems are systemic in part, yet states that blacks must be articulate and accomplished, to gain the respect of whites. The responsibility to develop these characteristics lies with blacks themselves—combined with more support for education from government. He feels that what happens to other blacks will only affect him "some," and when he talks about his intelligence and ability to communicate, he indicates that these are qualities that set him apart from many blacks.

Lee is one of the few students to hone in on the anti-Semitic rhetoric of Farrakhan. Other students, like Clifford Apprey of Brooks College (profiled in chapter 2), claim that Farrakhan has been misunderstood, and that anti-Semitic is an unfair characterization of his words. Lee, like Matthew Moore of Whelan (whose views were discussed in chapter 4), is concerned that blacks demonstrate the same fairness that they demand from whites, an idea not embraced by many in his cohort.

Laura Womack—Windsor University

The next student, Laura Womack, also has a limited racial group identity—not because of her experiences, as in Lee's case—but because of her mixed ancestry. She poignantly expresses the impossibility of her situation—having to choose between two very different worlds, and being accepted in neither. Laura Womack is the daughter of a Japanese mother and an African-American father. She is from the Southwest, and grew up in an area that was extremely intolerant of minorities. Laura is active in philanthropic activities in the community as well as political ones. One of her major activities is the organization of factory workers in the rural areas that surround the town.

Laura remembers well when she became aware that her African-American heritage was more significant in the eyes of others than her Japanese background. Her fifth grade teacher was conducting a count of ethnic students in the class. Laura raised her hand on both the Asian- and African-American count: "All the kids laughed at me. I remember crying and the teacher is telling me, 'no, you're black.' From that point on I've always put black on my application."

At about this age, Laura and her sister were called "dirty niggers" at a public pool. Several white girls told them to get out of the pool because they did not want their "dirty, greasy hair" in the pool. Then they spat upon them and forced them to leave. Laura was hurt, angry, and humiliated by this incident and the memory of it still causes her voice to tremble.

This was only one of many racial incidents in Laura's life. Her family joined, and then left, a predominantly white church because of the way members treated them. While doing a community service project that involved rehabilitating homes, Laura was confronted by one of the clients:

> She was an older white woman. I was the only person of color in that group. And she looked straight at me and said, "Why'd y'all bring a colored girl?" And I said, Oh, my God. I didn't know how to react. All of these thoughts went through my mind. I thought, should I say anything? I just went and stood outside for a while. She was so old.

Even her mother sometimes makes racist statements. She does not consider Laura and her sister black. She often says, "don't do that," meaning that they are doing something she considers black:

Like if we laugh loud, that's a black thing. Or if we, I still do this—she teaches me to cover my mouth when I laugh because that's [laughing without covering your mouth] unladylike. She tells us, "Don't act like the rest of those black kids—you're Japanese, too." Now she's beginning to realize how we feel 'cause we're always hurt every time she says that. She doesn't realize how the rest of society has labeled us and how we have come—aligned ourselves with African-Americans also.

She says her father is also guilty of making racist statements about Asians. Her mother responds in Japanese to her father when he does this, so Laura is not sure what she is saying. Her mother was disowned by her family for marrying her father. They are now separated, and Laura is doing research on marriages between Japanese women and American men. The women, she says, were rebelling against Japanese traditions. The men were seeking a submissive woman to bring back to the United States. Laura is not sure that this was her father's motivation, but she asserts that he is chauvinistic.

In spite of her experiences, Laura says she has a number of friends who are white, at least three of whom she considers close. Laura thinks about what she has in common with other blacks fairly often, and likes the term "Afro-Asian" to describe herself:

I write black because I know the politics behind it. I know that some people will feel that if you identify yourself as being mixed, you're trying to stray away from some of the stigma attached to being black. And I understand all of that. And I'm not trying to do that, I just feel that when I say I'm black to somebody I want to say "but I'm Japanese, too." I feel like I'm chopping off my mother and half of myself in saying that.

Laura feels that what happens to other blacks will affect her some. She complains that the talk shows misrepresent multiracial views because they always seem to have people that want to assimilate into one culture or the other. Laura thinks that in this country there is a black identity. She is now taking a comparative course on race relations in Brazil and the United States. This course has enlightened her about the role of race in other countries:

Taking that course has made me realize how blacks in other countries differ, where there is no equivalent to the NAACP. People don't organize around race. I think here we do—and there is a black identity. There is something that people organize around. I think it comes out of being racially oppressed. Discrimination forms a political identity.

Like many of the other students, Laura associates conservatives with the Republican Party. She also associates being conservative with being white and affluent. Moderates can align themselves with either party, but she thinks they tend to be liberal. Although Laura is liberal on most moral and cultural issues, she believes that the heart of a liberal ideology is justice and equality. Justice and equality are much more important to Laura than liberty, which she feels makes her a liberal.

Laura supports affirmative action, and finishes the statement on why blacks may not do well in life with "because of the history of discrimination in this country, and how institutions have forced them to the bottom of society." Government's role in ensuring racial equality should be to continue affirmative action initiatives. In her view, government should spend more on education, welfare, and crime prevention, and less on defense and prisons.

Laura believes that discrimination is at the root of the problems in the black community. The end result of the experience of discrimination is low self-esteem. She believes young people have internalized negative images of themselves, which leads to hopelessness and destructive behavior. People are "stuck in this stagnant pool where they can't move out of it."

For Laura, involvement of students such as herself is the solution. They should organize people in the community to lobby for resources. Mentoring by college students may also help boost the self-image of young people. She says, "We have to lobby and stop people like Newt Gingrich." Students are too apathetic and are not taking advantage of their power to change things.

She is a registered Democrat and voted for Clinton in the 1992 election. When asked to name the most influential black leader today, Laura could not think of anyone. She has mixed views about Louis Farrakhan. On the one hand, she disapproves of his statements about Jewish-Americans. On the other hand, she reads of some positive contributions the Nation makes to black communities.

Lee Vinson and Laura Womack both talk about the need for more and better educational opportunities for blacks, and mentoring and volunteerism as strategies for black empowerment. Lee approached the black identity question with caution, saying that it was about "shared experiences." He also mentioned that multiracial people should be given the opportunity to identify with more than one racial or ethnic group. Laura, a multiracial person, stated flatly that black identity was built on shared experiences of discrimination, not on a common history or a shared set of cultural practices. Black identity is not all-encompassing for either of them, if it is based on a fairly narrow range of experiences. In spite of this limited racial group identity, they are both very liberal. Their liberalism comes from an ideological commitment to justice, which may come from a perception that being black means more to others than it should.

A Legacy of Liberal Activism

Lela Riley—Benedict University

Lela Riley is from a rural community in her state, and attends Benedict on an athletic and academic scholarship. The area in which she grew up has a rich history dating back to slavery in which her ancestors played a prominent role. Stories she has heard about the struggles and triumphs of people in her community and the leadership and wisdom of her ancestors anchors Lela, and endows her with a sense of duty to help other blacks. She comes from a family of matriarchs. Her great-grandmother, grandmother, and mother reared her. These women continue the family legacy of community involvement, evidenced by her grandmother's membership in three civic organizations. They have passed these sensibilities on to Lela, who works with the homeless and serves as a mentor to children in impoverished neighborhoods.

Lela first became aware of racial differences in the first grade when she was transferred from a class for students with learning disabilities to a class for gifted students. She wondered why all the students in the first class were black, while all the students in the second class, with the exception of herself, were white. She says that just as she was misdiagnosed as learning disabled, other black students may suffer the same fate. Her mother and grandmother challenged the diagnosis, which led to a reevaluation and the conclusion that she was gifted.

Lela thinks about what she shares with other blacks just "once in a while," because she finds little in common with the majority of blacks at Benedict:

> I really like being out in the community, and I'm into politics. I really like to know what's going on. Especially at an HBCU [historically black college or university], people don't view you the same way. If you like theater, if you like going to dramas, if you like going to operas and stuff—it's not like, I mean if you're not into rap, or if you're not really down—like going to all these parties and whatever it's like they look at you differently. I don't have a problem with that but it's, I mean it's there, it's truth, you know?

She says that what happens to other blacks affects her a lot; however, while she knows something links all blacks, she does not know what it is:

> Anytime you go somewhere, when I go somewhere, when I see a lot of black folks, I'm going to go out of my way to speak to them—because, you know, just to see someone who looks like you, even though you might differ, you still have something in common.

When asked if she has ever experienced racial discrimination, Lela answers, "I can't say directly, but maybe indirectly." Then she immediately remembers a series of incidents that may have been more direct encounters with discrimination, the first of which is a job experience she had at sixteen as the only black worker in a fast-food restaurant:

> The manager, she would always just keep on bugging [being upset, antagonistic], she wasn't the operator, she owned the place, and she kept on bugging me and being hard on me. And I was playing volleyball, [working] a part-time job and going to school. She would make me clean the walls and stuff. I think the reason I stayed was to show her

that whatever you can say or you can do I can still go on. I ended up assistant manager when I turned seventeen, my senior year. It didn't happen to any other kids that worked there.

The second incident occurred while she was attending a predominantly white high school with a history of racial tensions. She was called a "nigger" by a fellow student:

In my math class, which [was on] computer systems, we were doing an equation and the guy called me a "nigger" for no reason. I was like, "OK." It was all because I knew the answer and we were working on it [the equation] together. I transferred back [to the school she had attended previously] after that.

Finally Lela admits that she and her friends are often ignored in restaurants and have to speak to the manager to get service. She says this could be racial but it is hard to be certain. For Lela, being called "black" is preferable to African-American. In light of these encounters, it is reasonable that she would answer the query about whether or not being black or American was most important to her with the question "Are we really American?" In order for blacks to claim the label American, Lela believes they must be treated like all other Americans.

In addition to thinking of the rich, Lela thinks of the Republican Party and welfare reform in connection with the term conservative. Moderates are more balanced, and liberals community oriented. Liberals want a peaceful environment, and will organize people at the grass-roots level to accomplish those ends. She considers her great-grandmother, grandmother, mother, and herself liberal. Her family's participation in grass-roots organizational efforts in the community attests to their belief that this is the best way to affect change. Lela is liberal on most moral and cultural issues. She began to think more about the rights of women when she became disturbed by the treatment of Lani Guinier after Clinton had nominated her for Attorney General for Civil Rights.

Lela thinks that problems in the black community stem from dysfunctional families and the loosening of the familial bond. The solution lies in educating blacks about the importance of family and practical strategies for creating and maintaining healthy families. She finishes the statement "In the United States, if black people don't do well in life, it is because" with "[of] the barriers built around our communities and within our families."

Lela supports affirmative action and believes that the government can help guarantee racial equality by keeping historically black colleges and universities (HBCUs) alive and helping to mobilize communities to work out their problems. Like most of the other students interviewed for this book, Lela believes government should increase funding for education. In her opinion, the government spends too little on welfare and crime; moreover, additional funds spent on crime should be on the rehabilitative end. She is worried about the "Contract with America" because of its impact on the homeless and financial aid for students: "It's not just a white and black issue, it's everyone's issue. Most students are on financial aid." She and her friends, most of whom are moderate, organized information sessions and a letter-writing campaign opposing the Republican "Contract."

A registered Democrat, Lela has voted once in the 1992 presidential election, for Clinton. She will be working for a candidate in the local city council election and encourages her friends to vote her way. When asked if there was a black politician she admired, she named Joycelyn Elders. She would characterize Louis Farrakhan only as "an effective speaker," and Jesse Jackson as "flaky."

Lela Riley joins the other young women in this chapter in her zeal for community activism and her belief that government has a large role to play in helping women on welfare and improving public education. The women here, as a rule, are much less individualistic than the young men, and favor organized efforts for change. While all the subjects mentioned strategies for changing the conditions of poor blacks, women seemed more concerned about quality of life issues, and less concerned about economic or entrepreneurial kinds of issues. Clearly the quality of life can be improved with more resources, but quality can also be improved by arming people with information and support so that they have more control over their lives.[3]

A Modern-Day "Harriet Tubman"*

Loren Terrell—Benedict University

Loren Terrell has already distinguished herself as a leader in campus politics. She was born and raised in the area, and is a serious young woman with strong political views. The daughter of professional parents, Loren has always attended integrated schools. She says that her parents have always made her aware of the political and social situation of African-Americans. When she was in the eighth grade, her classmates called her "Harriet Tubman" because even at that age she talked about racial issues.

Loren believes she experienced racism for the first time in junior high school. In the ninth grade, she ran for class president and was considered the favorite to win. However, administrators at the school eliminated her from the race saying that she had missed a meeting about which she had not been informed. They then sent a letter to her parents saying she was not eligible because they lived outside the district. To Loren's mind, the administrators could not accept a black student being class president. Loren said the memory of this incident was "so very vivid" in her mind:

> My parents say, "Don't ever give up." So I went to a counselor, a white counselor. She was like, "I don't know what I can do." I went [to the teacher's classroom responsible for the election] and said, "What do you mean I can't run? You must be crazy! I'm going to walk down that aisle and run anyway!" I went to the extreme for a while. I didn't call my parents initially, but after I got home I told them.

They let her run and she won the election. However, the Superintendent sent a letter to her parents after the election requesting that they move into the district. This experience convinced Loren that whites are capable of conspiring to keep blacks down.

Loren thinks about being black "all the time," and would like to get over being embarrassed by the behavior of other blacks. Being Amer-

---

*Harriet Tubman (1820–1913), escaped slavery and returned to the South to lead more than three hundred slaves to freedom via the Underground Railroad.

ican and black are both equally important to Loren; however, a "common history" is what unites blacks as an ethnic group. She is concerned about what she perceives as apathy on the part of her peers. It "amazes her" that her peers are so unaware. As the organizer of many campus events, Loren is frustrated when students seem reluctant to contribute to causes at Benedict even when she is giving them a lot of entertainment value for their contribution. She notes that they seem more willing to pay larger sums for smaller events at the majority-white institutions in the area. Loren says this shows that "white ice is still colder than black ice."

Conservatives, in Loren's mind, are close-minded. They are more likely to be Republicans than Democrats. Moderates "sit on the fence." She has problems with the term "liberal," and doubts that it has any meaning in contemporary politics. Loren has a male cousin who is also a feminist, which is as close as she can come to a description of a liberal. She thinks of herself as a "radical liberal."

In Loren's view, problems in the black community stem from "hopelessness—not being able to see a way out." She does not, however, place all the blame on society:

> Of course society has a role to play in it. It's just so difficult now to continue to pass the buck. It has to be a point in our lives where we start to take responsibility for our own actions. But at the same time, just being where I am, and I know sometimes I feel hopeless, I know someone else who hasn't had the opportunities that I've had—I can see how easy it would be just to give up.

The solution is to "help people become more self-reliant." Loren thinks that welfare is attractive to some people because job opportunities are limited:

> I know many people who are on welfare—and that's not the thing. But you know they make more money on welfare than they do getting a job sometimes, you know? I mean, where is the balance? Most of these people are not looking, they don't want handouts, not the ones I know anyway.
> *How would we help them become more self-reliant?*
> They have to know what's out there, what's available to them, be-

cause a lot of times they don't know. Like, some may not know
that as pregnant mothers they can get aid to help them go to
school to try to better themselves.

Whose responsibility is that?

It's definitely ours. If we have to go in there and pick somebody up
and bring them by the neck and bring them out—it's our responsibility.

When asked to say if she agreed, disagreed, or was neutral on affirmative action, Loren replied:

I can say I agree and disagree. I'm one that I think we need reparations.
I'm for that. They give Jews reparations—why not us? But at the same
time there are certain things we can do for ourselves. Like I was saying
before, we can't continue to pass the buck. It's a Catch-22, you know?
If we're on the same playing field, or if the race starts out even, it's one
thing. But if you are twenty spaces ahead of me and I have to catch up,
I'm not going to catch up.

Loren thinks government should increase education and welfare
spending. She believes the government spends too little on welfare
because "a lot of people who need it are probably not getting it." The
government spends too much on prisons and not enough on rehabilitation.

On moral and cultural issues, Loren is pro-choice and very tolerant of homosexuality. She is neutral on premarital sex and having
children out of wedlock. An active feminist in her community, Loren
feels that women do too much for which they receive little or no
credit. She is registered to vote and considers herself an Independent.
In the 1992 presidential election, she voted for Lenora Fulani. She encourages her friends and acquaintances to vote, and is a volunteer for
several local and state politicians. When asked which politician she
admired, Loren replied that she would have to "go old school" and
name Barbara Jordan and Maxine Waters. (Barbara Jordan was active, but ill at the time of this interview.) Loren does not think that
blacks have any viable leadership, and considers Jesse Jackson, Al
Sharpton, and Clarence Thomas "jokes." She compares them unfa-
vorably to Fannie Lou Hamer, about whom she says, "She wasn't re-

ally flamboyant, but you could feel her spirit. Even in just reading about her and seeing her in some videotapes, you could just feel her presence. And you knew that she was for real. And that's what's important to me."

Loren Terrell is an advocate for change, participating in local and state political campaigns, always with a Democratic candidate, and volunteering in poor communities. She declined to elaborate on what she meant by calling Jackson, Sharpton, and Thomas "jokes"; however, her statements indicate a longing for the era of protest politics, when there was less posturing and more direct action.

Summary

These young black students represent various ways of dealing with identity and integration. Lawrence Sims, integrated at an early age, wrestled with racial group identity, and resolved the crisis by embracing a liberal-radical political philosophy. Liz Thompson and Lana Tolliver, integrated during their teen years, are sure about their black identities. Both are also certain that the alienation they feel in majority-white situations is an indication of the cavernous cultural and political gap between whites and blacks in America.

The racial group identity of Lynn Stevens and Leah Somers was fashioned in the fires of economic struggle and painful self-doubt. Their political attitudes are traditional in the sense that government is seen as the source of both African-American problems and solutions. On moral and cultural issues, both women are less liberal than on issues of affirmative action and government spending. The most recent discussion about politics that Leah had with her friends was about the effect the Republican "Contract with America" would have on the black community. Their main concerns revolved around welfare reform and proposed policies on teenage pregnancies that would require teen mothers to remain in the household with their parents. There is little likelihood that Lynn or Leah would ever need welfare benefits. Yet these are the concerns of people that Lynn and Leah know and care about. The triple bind of race, gender, and class has been tightened by their experience at Windsor University, and may ultimately affect their allegiance to an exclusively racial political agenda. In the next and final chapter, the four themes revealed by these young leaders will be revisited with an eye toward understanding political possibilities and prospects for the "integration generation."

6

The Tie That Binds and Redeems
Negotiating Race in the Post–Civil Rights Era

Members of the post–civil rights generation are discovering that confronting race in an era without extreme conditions of racial segregation and oppression is a thorny enterprise. The rise of the black middle class has introduced the confounding element of class into the racial equation, and overt signs of racial segregation and subjugation are nearly nonexistent. Young black women are becoming aware of the double bind of race and gender, and want gender issues on the black political agenda. Race can no longer occupy front and center on the political stage—the "integration generation" must make room for class and gender, and a host of other once-peripheral issues such as multiracial classifications and black nationalism.

The salience of race is a constant throughout the various forms of identity and attitudes encountered within these pages. Some of the experiences related here were written about more than fifty years ago by Drake and Cayton. In *Black Metropolis* ([1945] 1962) they describe the racial tensions that erupted in Chicago over swimming areas along Lake Michigan and in the parks. Laura Womack, the young "Afro-Asian" woman, recalls being spat upon and running away from a public pool in her hometown. Public spaces of recreation and leisure remain points of racial contestation. E. Franklin Frazier ([1957] 1965) wrote that the middle class were more race-conscious than any other class—and so they are here. All of the Republican race men are from middle- to upper-class families. Frazier also wrote that southerners, particularly middle-class southerners, were more politically conservative than their northern counterparts. Here, the traditionally conservative and moderate students are mostly southerners.

These familiar patterns, however, are superimposed on a radically altered cultural and political background. Drake and Cayton, and Frazier were writing when African-Americans held few political offices, and most were relegated to working-class occupations. Media images of blacks were scarce, except in black-owned newspapers, and Americans could not even conceive of a multiracial citizen. Today, media images of blacks are everywhere, adding to the confusion about whether or not racism remains a problem. Benjamin DeMott (1995) argues that Hollywood images of black-white friendships such as the ones in *White Men Can't Jump* and *Regarding Henry* lull Americans into believing that blacks enjoy equal status with whites. If the fantasy friendships in the movies are part of the problem in facing up to the race issue, the reality of blacks with the power to influence entire industries—witness Oprah Winfrey's Book Club and the boom in the publishing business—complicates the issue even more.

The post–civil rights generation is witnessing and participating in an era when African-Americans are both defying and reinforcing stereotypes. Tiger Woods is much more than a phenomenal golfer—his mental toughness, cool exterior, and resistance to racial categorization makes him the embodiment of much of what perplexes young blacks. Morgan Stone, Lela Riley, Laura Womack, Charles Gaston, Clifford Apprey, Carol Changa, Carl Franks, and Liz Thompson all talked about feeling constrained by common notions of what it means to be black. Yet every one of them, and all the others here, believe that there is unity in black history, and in the collective responsibility of the black "haves" to help the black "have nots." In majority-white environments, the racial "tie that binds" grows tighter. In majority-black environments, it comforts and redeems the individual within, freeing each one to discover his or her own truths about race.

Majority-White Spaces and Black Folks' Places

Students in majority-white universities talked about small things, and large things, that made them feel disaffected from their campus communities. Several mentioned an aspect that may underlie some of this disaffection—a perception that whites do not recognize, respond to, or respect the perspectives that they have acquired through their experiences as African-Americans. An example was Lana Tolliver's disappointment at the inability of her white teacher to understand her rage over the Rodney King beating. Some students said they believed that blacks and whites could never coexist, and point to continuing residential segregation as proof.

African-Americans exhaust tremendous reserves of energy coping with the attendant problems of blackness. Leaving behind this tiresome truth was a driving force behind the civil rights movement. However, association with whites has not brought the hoped-for diminishment of race. It may have increased it. If blacks are unaware of racial identity in majority- or all-black environments, they become acutely aware of it in majority-white environments. Without exhausting the full range of possibilities as to why this is so, the following ideas are worth discussing, mainly because they have been bandied about in the literature on identity politics:

(1) Rejection by whites on a social level triggers a retreat into one's blackness;
(2) Black students are compensating for feelings of inferiority;
(3) Feelings of alienation, experiences with racism, and the failure of institutions to address these problems;
(4) A political and social climate that constrains discussion of, or protestation against, racism.

Writers such as Steele (1990) have explored the first and second suppositions, but there is little empirical evidence to support such notions. Comfort may be found, as Ilene Philipson (1991) has noted, in the collective bosom of others who share a feeling of alienation. What is puzzling about these particular explanations for the resurgence of identity politics is that, if they are correct, why is this so? Further, if black students are feeling inferior, why and how did these feelings originate? More than one student questioned his or her innate ability to handle the academic demands at majority-white institutions. This self-doubt was clearly linked to feelings of alienation, and at least one study provides evidence supporting this linkage (Allen, Epps, and Haniff 1991). In other words, an atmosphere that arouses feelings of inadequacy is not ideal for achieving academic excellence. The third and fourth suppositions are supported by ample evidence. Conflicts between black and white students are occurring nationwide, which shows how much work needs to be done to get at the source of racial animosities.

The idea that a majority-black environment may be more conducive to expressing ideological differences is an unexpected finding. However, if black students are isolated in majority-white schools, it makes sense that black unity would be promoted. Black students at majority-white institutions are walking a racial tightrope. They take great pains to acknowledge that whites cannot be responsible for improving conditions in poor black communities. While some maintain that you cannot expect your enemy to rescue you, and others believe that it is simply black folks' job to fix things, they *all* want blacks to do more to help poor blacks. These students are hypersensitive to the stereotype of blacks as freeloaders, whiners, and dependent on government largesse. They have been forced to feel embarrassed over affirmative action in college admissions, although they seem completely convinced that public education is inadequate in poor communities.

In majority-white environments, many black students are likely to embrace a black identity to protect themselves from feeling that they do not belong. Solidarity with other black students then becomes an essential survival tool. Clifford Apprey said when he saw another black student in a class at the private preparatory school he attended, he felt that they had to "make it together."

As the 1980s progressed, racial tensions on college campuses all across the country increased, marked by increasing verbal and physical assaults involving black and white students. An examination of only the most publicized incidents on campuses using the Lexis-Nexis newspaper database, yielded ninety-six occurrences from 1980 through 1995. One of the most symbolic episodes was one in which two white students, wielding guns, donned Ronald Reagan masks and attacked a black student in his dormitory room at the University of

Texas. Many incidents revealed gross insensitivity by white students. For example, many episodes involved white students appearing in blackface and Afro wigs at parties or during pledging activities. This insensitivity to the power of racial symbols to inflict pain upon black students shows that institutions have failed to devise effective strategies to deal with racial issues.

One outcome of this institutional failure is that black enrollment at historically black colleges and universities (HBCUs) is on the rise. As Figure 6.1 indicates, before 1986, enrollment at HBCUs was holding steady. Since 1986, enrollment has dramatically increased. It is interesting that twenty of the ninety-six incidents reported in the national media occurred in 1987. This is about the same time that enrollment began increasing at HBCUs. While historically black colleges and universities remain crucial to the education of African-Americans and should always be supported, it is less than ideal when they become a refuge from the hostile environment that exists on some majority-white campuses.

_ According to data compiled by The Prejudice Institute at Towson

Figure 6.1. Fall Enrollment in Historically Black Colleges and Universities, 1970–93

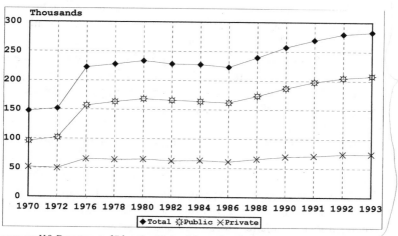

SOURCE: U.S. Department of Education, National Center for Education Statistics. Statistics from 1970 and 1972 obtained from: *Fact Book on Education in the South*, Southern Reginal Education Board, Atlanta. Ga., publisher.

State University in Baltimore, one of every four minority students is victimized for reasons of prejudice at least once during the school year. Dr. Howard J. Erlich, codirector of the Institute and a principal investigator in the study, writes that "the most common forms of ethnoviolence are acts of verbal aggression" (Erlich 1995). These acts become more potent as they are related to other members of the group, creating what Erlich has termed "covictims"—people who experience the same distress as the victim upon hearing about the incident. Feagin and Sikes (1994) call this aspect of racism—the coupling of one's own experiences with racism with the experiences of other members of the group—the "cumulative effect" of racism. When Liz Thompson of Woodson talked about her friend whom the Klan terrorized, it was as if she herself had been part of the experience. On one majority-white campus, more than half (59 percent) of the black students had experienced verbal assaults by whites on campus, and an amazing 81 percent said that they did not report all incidents of racial harassment to authorities (D'Augelli and Hershberger 1993:76).

Although many institutions have attempted to promote racial harmony by providing ethnic studies courses and cultural centers, more needs to be done. A 1990 report by the United States Commission on Civil Rights mentions that universities have failed on several levels to quell growing racial resentment. First, most institutions do not respond swiftly and firmly to violations against minority students. Second, white Generation X students, because they lack an understanding of the history and rationale that created affirmative action programs, feel resentful of minority students. Some are annoyed that blacks are encouraged to celebrate their ethnicity while doing the same seems taboo for whites. White Generation Xers support egalitarian principles in the abstract, but balk at affirmative action (Sonner and Mayer 1997). There are few mechanisms, such as mandatory seminars or courses, for students to develop an informed opinion. Third, there are more minority students on white campuses, and they are more likely to unite in making demands for equal treatment. When minority students protest or make demands as a group, white students are resentful.

The hope that integration and time would usher in a new era of race relations has not been fulfilled, in part because the post–civil rights generation has experienced a different kind of racism but one just as damaging as the kind experienced by their parents. The problem is that this racism is more difficult to identify, provide evidence of, and even more painful to acknowledge. *Symbolic* and *aversive* racism are two strains of racism that have evolved over the last decade. According to Brigham (1993), the feeling that minorities eschew values such as individualism and personal responsibility charges symbolic racism. Malice toward blacks causes aversive racism that remains in the realm of the unconscious. This kind of racism is manifested by an avoidance of blacks and a rationalization of this behavior (Brigham 1993). It is not surprising that in the face of these obstacles racial group membership continues to be salient.

The psychology of nigrescence literature argues that black identity is realized during a five-stage process. The "encounter" stage, in which the individual first glimpses the meaning of racial group membership, seems the most critical. It is often not a "stage," but a moment in time. Much like spiritual enlightenment, it is powerful—and may present itself during a spectacular event, in the middle of a quiet exchange, while meeting the stare of another, or in tiny increments of insight. Cornell Hall vividly recalls the humiliation of his mother by a store clerk, related in Chapter 2—his "encounter" moment. He was in the seventh grade at the time, and later says that his "problack" identity phase began in the eighth grade. The Rodney King incident sent Lana Tolliver into a tailspin, after which she began reading about activists in the civil rights and black power movements. Lawrence Sims was shocked by a white schoolmate's snide comment about another black's financial dependence on paying students. The comment was short— just an aside—but for Lawrence it spoke volumes about how whites felt about him. Some of the students interviewed had their "encounter" moment in early childhood, but most did not have it until much later. Moreover, they were less prepared than their parents for the sometimes difficult emotions that this moment can induce. In majority-white institutions, this reality that they have come to know is not honored, propelling them toward a stronger black identity.

Historically black colleges have become more desirable for some students and parents because they are places where blacks are not haunted by the specter of affirmative action or racial stereotyping. There is colorism and classism to deal with in some instances, but to many, these "isms" are preferable to racism. Moreover, most historically black institutions are located in or near cities with large black populations and a variety of social and cultural outlets. For some in the post–civil rights generation, the tradition and history of these institutions anchors them and provides them with a place to develop an authentic sense of self. All the students interviewed at HBCUs told me that they would not trade anything for the experience—especially those who had spent most of their lives in majority-white schools.

Black Nationalism and the Young Black Republicans

The young men who are active members of the Republican Party represent a small percentage of young black college students.[1] No exact figures exist on the number of young black Republicans in Project 21, a black organization sponsored by the Republican Party, so at this point we cannot gauge the real strength of Republican Party ideology in the integration generation. The 1996 presidential vote suggests that the Republican Party has not attracted enough African-Americans to register on the political radar screen. However, the young Republicans interviewed here are questioning the utility of dependence on federal governmental remedies and other ideas that political liberals support. Their experiences tell them that much remains wrong with race relations, but they have little confidence in the liberal strategies of the past.

The similarities in the ideologies espoused by Louis Farrakhan and the Republican Party are obvious. Both the Republicans and Farrakhan preach self-reliance, the development of entrepreneurial skills, and traditional lifestyles. Why, then, don't these young men just become members of the Nation of Islam? Some claimed disagreement with Islam as a religion, and others never fully explained why the Republican Party was a better match. Perhaps even they do not understand why they have chosen to be Republicans; however, they give us some clues. These young men share middle- to upper-class socioeconomic status, and come from traditional two-parent households where the father is the most influential parent in shaping their political ideas. The availability of resources has meant that their life experiences have been similar to those of middle-class white students. The traditional roles played by their fathers are also similar to that of their white counterparts. Yet they are acutely aware of the circumstances of other members of their race, and how racial stereotypes affect them. It is possible that these young men are simply trying to reconcile the conflict produced by their class, their ideas about the role of men in society, and their racial group status. As young men of means, they are not comfortable with the urban and working-class makeup of the Nation of Islam, but appreciate the empowering message of Farrakhan. The Republican Party, while not a perfect fit, is a better fit than the Democratic Party. In their view, the Democrats project the idea that blacks are incapable of changing their own situation and controlling their fate. The Democrats also support nontraditional lifestyles that are problematic for young men from traditional households.

The Not-So-New South: Regional Influences on Racial Attitudes

Although scholars debate the idea of the exceptionalism of southern politics, these students show that growing up in the South, particularly in small towns and rural communities, influences political attitudes and perceptions about the meaning of "being black." They were more moderate and less wedded to the notion of a definitive black identity than students from larger urban settings. They also reported more overt and vicious encounters with racism than students from other regions.

How is it that a region so fraught with racial conflict could avoid producing more liberal or nationalistic young blacks? Perhaps the fear of racial stereotyping, so pervasive, humiliating, and oppressive in the South, causes them to eschew rigid conceptions of blackness. Southerners, overall, have strong beliefs about individualism and the obligation of family—as opposed to government—to take care of each other. Southern blacks share this belief, perhaps more intensely because of the realization that one of the most powerful stereotypes of blacks is one of irresponsibility and welfare dependency.

Lynn, the young woman at Windsor from a small town in the South, talked about the virulent nature of racism in her community. She also talked about her apprehension about confirming stereotypes of blacks as incapable of majoring in the "hard" sciences. Because of her perception that blacks are considered better at the humanities and social sciences, she attempted to avoid these subject areas. The link between blacks' awareness of, and resistance to, stereotypes may explain why they express more moderate political attitudes and less fixed ideas regarding a black identity.

Race and Gender

Most of the young women interviewed here talked about the tension between gender and racial identities. The concern about issues of gender equality is particularly relevant for them because of Farrakhan's influence on members of the integration generation. The Nation of Islam believes that women have a more traditional role to play in the struggle for racial equality, and practically ignores gender issues such as domestic abuse, sexual exploitation, and the double bind of race and sex discrimination.

Most of the women interviewed here were doing well in school, yet some expressed doubts about their ability to succeed. More than one said that she often wondered whether a perceived slight was because of her gender status or racial group membership. On predominantly white campuses, there are twice as many black women as black men, and black women seem to fare better academically. However, black men have higher aspirations and choose more competitive fields than black women (Allen, Epps, and Haniff 1991:251).

Young black women cannot avoid being aware of the various stereotypes of black women. More than one complained about the exploitation of black women in "gangsta" rap lyrics and videos. They also resented portrayals of black women in movies, with some specifically citing Spike Lee films as portraying black women as either weak or emasculating. They believe that these media images contribute to the varying perceptions of black women as morally loose, or as self-less caregivers, or ruthlessly ambitious and aggressive. This belief is supported by a study of images of black women held by white college students. White students characterized black women as loud, talka-tive, aggressive, intelligent, straightforward, argumentative, and lack-ing in self-control. The most important finding, however, is that they rated positive traits as less positive in black women than in white women. Similarly, they rated negative traits as less negative, because their *expectations* conformed to negative stereotypes of black women (Weitz and Gordon 1993).

Black women need black leadership to include their struggle in the plan for black empowerment. The black male has serious obstacles to overcome, but the black female is also in crisis. Andrew Grant-Thomas (1996) argues that while the black male is quantifiably worse off in the criminal justice system, the black female is more likely to be living in poverty. Additionally, the black experience, past and present, is often related in terms of an exclusively male experience (Grant-Thomas 1996). Women in the integration generation are likely to be much less reluctant to contest the continuing emphasis on the black man's story.

Shared Sentiments

Several common responses to questions merit discussion. The first was the nearly universal respect, if not approval of, Minister Louis Farrakhan, leader of the Nation of Islam. While it is entirely possible that, as Stanley Crouch has argued, these young people embrace Far-rakhan "for the same reason teenagers go to hear the most obnoxious rock bands—to soak themselves in self-righteous alienation and mud-dled outrage" (Crouch 1995:71), this may only be wishful thinking. Most of the students interviewed here are well past the stage where they find it necessary to attempt to free themselves from emotional and psychological attachments to parents by dressing strangely and listening to aggravating music. Farrakhan may be providing explanations, however apocryphal, for these students' very real feeling of alienation. The black media can be credited with setting much of the agenda in the black community. Louis Farrakhan appeared on the *Arsenio Hall*[2] late-night interview show in 1994, and has been featured in several black magazines more than once. In an article in one of these magazines, *Emerge,* it was reported that two respected television news shows, the *MacNeil/Lehrer NewsHour* and ABC's *Nightline* edited a speech given by Minister Farrakhan that distorted the meaning of his words (Curry 1994). This kind of "inside story" supports black suspicions of media misrepresentation.

Time magazine, in its startling 1994 cover story on Farrakhan— "Ministry of Rage"—reported on the Nation of Islam's record of success in rehabilitating drug users and criminals. Yet the writer announced with astonishment that a poll of 504 African-Americans revealed that 67 percent believed Farrakhan was an effective leader (Henry 1994). Clearly college students are not the only segment of the black population with whom Farrakhan's rhetoric resonates. While it is troubling that blacks have not critically assessed Farrakhan's ideas, their discontent with continuing inequalities should be acknowledged in any discussion of Farrakhan's influence.

Media Images of Blacks

All the students in this survey complained about the images of blacks in the news media, television, and film. They believe that criminal activity in the black community is too often the lead story on local news shows. Some believe news reporters deliberately find blacks to interview who fit their viewers' stereotypical idea of what blacks look like and how they speak. Research by Franklin Gilliam (Gilliam and Simon 1996) suggests that images of black perpetrators in television news programs are sufficiently powerful to change racial attitudes. Especially troubling is the finding that it is the white liberal who is most susceptible to this manipulation, not the white conservative (Gilliam and Simon 1996). These students are cognizant of the power of these negative images because they experience the fallout—especially the young men. When they see fear on the faces of people they meet on elevators, they know that it comes from believing that most criminals are African-American.

The Fox Network-sponsored lineup of black programs was often the first response to the question about blacks in the media. Some members of the Young Black Republicans became apoplectic in their criticism of two Fox sitcoms, *Living Single* and *Martin*. They believe that the four young black women featured in *Living Single* are all stereotypes, and that Martin Lawrence, a stand-up comedian and the star of *Martin* is a twentieth-century Stepin' Fetchit.[3]

Some were bored with film plots about black gangs and street life, while others thought that these stories were more acceptable than ones that portrayed blacks as having overcome problems of poverty and inequality. Men and women felt that black female characters were the most offensive in current films, and had not evolved much past the "Mammy" roles of the pre–World War II era and the "Jezebel" roles of the 1960s blaxploitation era. These reflections on the entertainment industry were interesting since many television sitcoms and movies named were highly successful and seen by many blacks. These students said that they supported movies directed by blacks about blacks, but sometimes felt let down by the lack of substance. Students critical of the television shows said that they hardly ever viewed them after a few initial tryouts, but they had friends who were loyal fans. The popularity of these programs and films prompts questions about the demographics of the audience. Do working-class blacks watch more television than middle-class blacks? Do educated blacks have different viewing habits than uneducated blacks? More research is required if we are to learn how class status affects reactions to stories or situations depicting lifestyles from which some black people are attempting to dissociate themselves.

Acknowledging Racism

Students responded to questions about experiences with racism with unexpected circumspection. They often first replied that they had never been victims of racism—usually adding "that I am *aware* of." After allowing a few moments of thoughtful silence, they might venture something that *might* have been tainted by racism. Sometimes the interview would move forward, only to have them ask to return to the question about experiences with racism. Several prefaced their stories with "I don't know if this is important" or, "I don't know if this happened because of race." One student, Carl Franks, emphasized that "he was not one to call racism at the drop of a dime." He also took great pains to explain to me how sometimes people make assumptions about blacks that are simply the result of logical shortcuts that all humans make to assess situations quickly.

This diffidence, mentioned in the earlier chapters, is probably due to sensitivity about complaints of racism being taken as excuses made for failures. Others have proposed that the fault lies with their middle-class parents who have not prepared them to deal with racism (Feagin and Sikes 1994:96). The shock of these encounters may make identification of racism more difficult, or encourage denial that these incidents ever took place.

These young African-Americans spoke consistently of the need for self-reliance and community-based strategies for solving black problems. They were clearly keen not to appear to be the kind of black person that sees racism everywhere. To acknowledge racism as a factor in their lives would be a sign of weakness, or an excuse for personal failure. Acknowledging racism can also mean admitting to limitations that are externally imposed. As Carl Franks pointed out, thinking that race is a factor is self-limiting. Making even the thought of racism an invitation to failure makes the racial tightrope these students walk more taut.

Black Leadership Crisis

Most revelatory among this group of young people was the lack of faith in the black political leadership. Many were harsh in their appraisal of black members of Congress, and not one of them mentioned the NAACP or the Urban League as viable black organizations. At least one student, Matthew Moore of Whelan University, did not see the paucity of black leadership as a problem. He felt that black political and economic empowerment should be decentralized—replaced by community leadership.

The Young Black Republicans have lost faith in the ability of most political leaders to think of solutions to problems in the community. They are certain that most lack credibility in powerful political circles. Some students mentioned the scandals that have plagued black politicians in recent years, but few expressed sympathy. As Cornell Hall of Barnett said, "they were not *representing* . . . you have be *above reproach.*"

The Mutability of Identity and Its Effects on Political Attitudes

The ideas and experiences of these young people suggest that some changes are on the political horizon. They resemble the civil rights generation in that they are mostly liberal on race issues and conservative on moral and cultural issues. The Republican race men are different in that they have attempted to fashion an ideological framework that can accommodate their racial group membership, class, and gender status. Experiences with racism had profound effects on some of these students, which may have been exacerbated by their attendance at majority-white universities. All the students want blacks to take more responsibility for improving conditions among the poorest in their group. The conservatives and moderates fault black behavior and leadership more than the liberals do. This willingness to be self-critical is a good thing, even if the criticism is not always accurate. We can look forward to more diversity of opinion and a broader discussion of racial problems and solutions taking place among members of this generation, especially—although somewhat surprisingly—among the growing numbers of black youth attending HBCUs.

Some of the opinions of these students are a reflection of a particular stage of life, but their frustration and alienation in majority-white environments should be taken seriously. Their stories reflect the failure of integration to promote racial understanding. The student leaders at Woodson all mentioned becoming more aware of race since their arrival at the university. Leah Somers believed, incredibly, that she might have experienced her intellectual peak at the tender age of seventeen.

Integration has not been an altogether negative experience for the students at Whelan. This was the one majority-white campus in which black and white students were observed walking together and lunching together. In an average of two to three days spent at each interview site, there were few observations of black and white students interacting at Woodson or Windsor. Black students at Whelan are involved in both black and white service organizations on campus and student government. All were moderate to conservative in their political attitudes, which is related to life in small towns and rural communities. It may also be linked to feeling less isolated in the larger university community. Just as the Republican race men believe that the historically black college environment allows black students the freedom to express more conservative views, a more comfortable majority-white environment may have the same effect. We should remember that although Whelan was clearly a more hospitable environment, only one student out of the six interviewed claimed to have any white friends.

One wonders what would happen if the more traditional conservatives—Carol Changa and Carl Franks, for example—were placed in a historically black college environment. What if the Republican race men were at Woodson or Windsor? Would their nationalism turn to radical liberalism? If we could transplant Lawrence Sims to Brooks or Barnett, would his radical liberalism become more traditional liberalism? Black identity is not necessarily fixed, but may be strengthened or weakened by environment, class, and experiences with discrimination.

Why should we care about how and why racial group identity is formed? One reason is that racial group identity is dominant in political decision making. Although sometimes advantageous, this can also result in exploitation of the group and the omission of problems or concerns that are crucial to the group's advancement. An example is the failure of traditional or fringe organizations (NAACP, Nation of Islam) to address gender and class issues in their black empowerment programs. Another problem is that racial divisions distract the citizenry from larger issues such as employment, economic policy, and health. Clearly people of color are more disadvantaged than whites in these areas, which helps to maintain racial cleavages and keeps public discussions about these issues at bay. Efforts to redirect the public's attention to areas that affect all citizens are consistently thwarted, because "playing the race card" is easy and effective. President Clinton, now putting racial healing on the agenda, first avoided facing racial issues head-on. It was a strategic move to alter his "problack" image, and it worked.

This book has raised as many questions as it has sought to answer. To what degree is the leadership in higher education responsible for perpetuating racial divisions? University officials have ample space to negotiate the elements contributing to the strengthening of black identity among the students interviewed here. Many university campuses support black theme dorms and separate graduations for black students in the name of recognizing cultural differences, yet fail to require students to take multicultural courses. Some universities refuse to guide black student organizations in the selection of speakers, and in the name of tolerance allow speakers on campus who not only have little to offer the students intellectually, but fan the flames of intolerance to boot. College and university administrators need to reassess their management of their multicultural student bodies, and find the courage to carry out policies and guidelines that will promote racial understanding.

Members of the "integration generation" will enter the twenty-first century with the issue of the color line still on the political agenda. Also on the agenda will be multiracial classifications, affirmative action, school integration, and black nationalism—and everything is up for review. The old frameworks are worn, and new ones must be built. The "tie that binds"—*being black*—has strands of history, music, family life, and discrimination. It both braces and constrains, and may ultimately expand to include others in its fold.

Appendix A
The Research Design

The purpose of this research is to discover how the post–civil rights generation thinks about racial group identity and political issues, and to explore connections between the two. The complexity and sensitivity of the subject called for in-person interviews, which have the advantage of allowing the researcher to pursue lines of questioning in response to the subject's answer. There is a suppleness to this method that is useful for uncovering aspects of a phenomenon that may remain hidden because of the necessary constraints imposed by other methods. The trust that can be established between the researcher and subject in an in-person interview is invaluable when encouraging subjects to define issues for themselves.

Several considerations determined the selection of sites for this research. One initial observation was that the resurgence of interest in black nationalism and Republican Party conservatism was occurring simultaneously. In light of this observation, it seemed logical to solicit students from both historically black and majority-white institutions. If all the subjects had come from one or the other, the inherent implications in the choice one makes to attend a majority-white or a historically black institution may have skewed the findings. Further, the Young Black Republican organizations on record at the Republican National Headquarters were all based at historically black colleges or universities, most of which are found in the South. In choosing the majority-white institutions, proximity to the chosen historically black institution was a primary consideration for several reasons: first, it would help control for the effects of locale; and second, it would be more manageable logistically. Table A.1 gives the demographic data on each site. All the institutions' and students' names have been changed to protect the identities of the students. The names of the majority-white institutions begin with "W," and those of the historically black institutions with "B."

After the sites were selected, administrators, faculty members in political science departments, or both, were contacted and asked to serve as intermediaries in selecting volunteers. The intermediaries solicited students who were considered leaders on campus—except members of the Young Black Republicans, whom we solicited directly. "Leaders" were defined as students holding office in one or more institutionally sanctioned organization, involved in one or more community service project, and in good academic standing. Since one of the main lines of inquiry involved the potential for black involvement in the Republican Party, we also directly solicited students who were organizers and members of Young Black Republican organizations for participation in this research. In the end, subjects were obtained through selective sampling and from the volunteers obtained by the intermediaries, and came from three historically black and three majority-white institutions. Twenty-

TABLE A.1
Demographic Data on Interview Sites

Woodson	Brooks	Windsor	Benedict	Whelan	Barnett
Majority-White Private	Historically Black Private	Majority-White Private	Historically Black Public	Majority-Public	Historically Black Private
Urban Setting in Large Southern City		Small Town Setting in the South		Urban Setting in Midsized Southern City	
Student Populations		Student Populations		Student Populations	
Total: 6,000* Black: 12%	Total: 2,600*	Total:6,207* Black: 8.4%	Total:4,070*	Total:21,523** Black: 16%	Total:5,324*
Subjects Interviewed		Subjects Interviewed		Subjects Interviewed	
5	2	5	5	5	2

* Undergraduate Only
**Undergraduate and Graduate

four respondents were interviewed for over two hours each. The sample includes residents of only ten states. The following is the regional classification employed that includes both the states in which the subjects reside, and additional states to prevent the identification of the subjects. Southern states included Virginia, North Carolina, South Carolina, Alabama, Tennessee, and Georgia. Northeastern states included New York, Connecticut, Massachusetts, Pennsylvania, and Rhode Island. Southwestern states included Texas, Arizona, and New Mexico, and the West included California, Oregon, and Nevada. An urban classification was assigned to any student who resided in a city of more than one million people. Rural communities had less than 30,000 residents, and small towns less than 200,000 residents.

A copy of the survey instrument is included in Appendix B. All the questions were asked in every interview. Sometimes a question led to other questions that were particular to that subject's experience or situation. These students were not asked questions that assessed their sophistication or knowledge of politics, mainly because this was not considered relevant to the research agenda. Many were political science majors, and all were engaged in activities that qualified them to be called student leaders. In answering the questions, the students revealed themselves to be about as sophisticated as most Americans.

The chapters are organized according to ideological groups, which are shown in Table A.2. In an effort to organize the data efficiently, the names of conservative students begin with "C," liberal students with "L," and moderate students with "M." The table below gives the criteria for determining the socioeconomic background of students, which is a modification of the 1995 poverty guidelines set by the Department of Health and Human Services. The students were not asked the incomes of their parents; however, income was estimated by occupational status. This method has several flaws: one, there was no way to determine the total number of dependents, since black families are often extended families, and parents are responsible for members outside the immediate family; two, there are some working-class occupations that pay middle- or upper-class incomes. Efforts were

TABLE A.2
Background and Ideological Chart of Interview Subjects

Conservatives (Republican Race Men)	Conservatives (Traditional)	Moderates	Liberals
Charles Gaston –Brooks Clifford Apprey –Brooks Chris Gray –Barnett Cornell Hall –Barnett	Curtis Foster –Benedict Conrad Terry –Benedict Corliss Bond –Whelan Carol Changa –Woodson Carl Franks –Windsor	Marie Potter –Woodson Marilyn Lacey –Whelan Michael Washington –Whelan Matthew Moore –Whelan Morgan Stone –Whelan Myra Mason Whelan	Lawrence Sims –Woodson Liz Thompson –Woodson Lana Tolliver –Woodson Lynn Stevens –Windsor Leah Somers –Windsor Lee Vinson –Windsor Laura Womack –Windsor Lela Riley –Benedict Loren Terrell –Benedict
Institution: Historically Black Private	Institution: Majority-White and Historically Black Public and Private	Institution: Majority-White and Historically Black Public and Private	Institution Majority-White and Historically Bkack Public and Private
Environment: Urban	Environment: Urban and Rural	Environment: Urban and Rural	Environment: Urban and Small Town
Household: Two-Parent	Household: Two-Parent	Household: Single-Parent (3) and Two-Parent (3)	Household: Single-Parent (6) and Two-Parent (3)
*Experiences with Discrimination: Mild to Moderate	Experiences with Discrimination: Mild to Moderate	Experiences with Discrimination: Mild	Experiences with Discrimination: Intense
Socioeconomic Status Middle to Upper Class	Socioeconomic Status Working to Upper Class	Socioeconomic Status Middle Class	Socioeconomic Status Poor to Middle Class
Gender: Men	Gender: Men and Women	Gender: Men and Women	Gender: Men and Women

*The intensity of experiences with racism was measured by gauging the emotionalism of the students' responses, whether or not the incident involved a verbal or physical threat, and whether or not racial epithets were used. The author acknowledges that what is an intense experience to one person may not be an intense experience to another; therefore, the first criterion is less objective. Recognizing individual perspectives, however, remains important, and should be reported as accurately as possible.

made to overcome these flaws by gathering information that might throw light on such situations and thereby permit us to make an accurate determination.

Criteria for Socioeconomic Classifications

Socioeconomic Strata	Occupation	Education	Income
Upper Class	Entrepreneurs Executives	College Degree Postgraduate Work	Over 50K
Middle Class	Managerial, professional, administrative, skilled craftsmen	College Jr Coll or Semiprofessional Training	35K–50K
Working Class	Service, semiskilled operatives, clerical	HS Diploma, Apprenticeships, Technical Training	15K–35K
Lower Class	Unskilled laborers, domestic and farm laborers	Some High School, Jr. High School Completion	15K and Under

Appendix B

Survey of Political Attitudes of Young African-Americans

I. Familial and Environmental Influences
   A. Family Background
      1. Where are you from originally? How did you make your decision to attend school here? What do you think about this (college, university)?
      2. Could you tell me a little about where you grew up? For example, was the neighborhood all or mostly black, or mostly white?
      3. What kind of work did your parents do?
      4. Do you have any siblings? How old are they? Have any of them attended college or are attending college now? What are their occupations?
      5. How would you describe your family's financial situation when you were growing up? What was your neighborhood like?
   B. Educational Background
      1. Was the elementary school you attended integrated?
      2. What about junior high or middle school? What was it like?
      3. And high school, what do you remember about your high school? Was it integrated? What year did you graduate?
      4. What kind of student were you in high school? What about now?

C. Church and Organizational Memberships
  1. Did your family attend church? What denomination? Was the church integrated? Were you active in church?
  2. Would you consider yourself religious? What about your family members?
  3. Were your parents active in any organizations outside of church?
  4. What about now? What organizations are you a member of?

II. Political Socialization

  A. Family
    1. What do the terms conservative, moderate, and liberal mean to you in regards to political views?
    2. How would you characterize your parents' political views? Are they conservative, liberal, moderate, or a combination of some sort?
    3. What about you? How would you define your views?
    4. Can you think of anyone who has influenced your views? What about events? Can you think of any events that have influenced your views?
    5. Were your parents, or any members of your family politically active? In what way?

  B. Friends
    1. Do any of your close friends have strong political views? How would you characterize those views?
    2. How many of your close friends are white?
    3. Do you and your friends ever discuss politics or political events? What has been the latest topic of discussion?

III. Strength of Group Identity

  A. Recognition of Racial Differences
    1. Do you remember when you first became aware of racial differences? For example, how old were you? Was it in the neighborhood, at school, or somewhere else?

  B. Experiences with Racism
    1. Have you ever experienced racial discrimination?

    2. Have you ever been called a name by a white person? If so, what was that name and how old were you at the time? Did you know what it meant? What was your response? Where did this occur?

    3. What about your family members and friends? Have they had any experiences of racial discrimination?

C. Racial Identity

    1. What do you prefer to be called, black, African American, or something else? Why?

    2. People differ in whether they think about being black— what they have in common with other blacks. What about you—do you think about this a lot, fairly often, once in a while, or hardly ever?

    3. Do you think what happens generally to black people in this country has anything to do with what happens in your life? If yes, will it affect you a lot, some, or not very much?

    4. Which would you say is most important to you—being *black*, being *American*, or are *both equally* important to you?

    5. Do you think there is such a thing as a black identity?

    6. Do you think that the civil rights movement made a difference in your life? If so, how? If not, why not?

    7. What do you think the larger society believes about black identity?

    8. What do you think about portrayals of blacks in the media?

    9. Can you think of any book or movie that you believe is an accurate portrayal of any aspect of black life?

IV. Attitudes on Issues Related to Race

    1. What factors do you believe contribute most to the social and economic state of poor black communities?

    2. How do you think problems in poor black communities can be solved most effectively?

    3. Do you believe that in the past five years things have improved, remained the same, or gotten worse for blacks?

For the following statements I would like for you to tell me whether you agree, disagree, or are neutral:

4. Because of past discrimination, minorities should be given special consideration when decisions are made about hiring applicants for jobs.

5. Job applicants should be judged solely on the basis of test scores and other individual qualities.

6. The government should not make any special effort to help blacks and other minorities because they should help themselves.

7. In the United States, if black people don't do well in life, it is because. . .

8. Do you think blacks will ever achieve full economic and social equality in your lifetime?

9. Do you think government should have a role in guaranteeing racial equality? If so, what do think it should be?

V. Political Attitudes

A. Attitudes on Government Spending

1. If you could influence the federal budget, in what areas would you increase spending? What are the areas in which you would decrease spending?

2. How do you feel about welfare spending? Does the government spend too much, too little, or is it about right?

3. What do you think about spending on crime? Does the government spend too much, too little, or is it about right?

B. Attitudes on Moral and Cultural Issues

1. How do you feel about abortion?

2. What do you think about homosexuality?

[Respondents are asked to place themselves on a scale from 1 to 10 with 1 symbolizing "intolerant" and 10 "very tolerant."]

3. What do you think about premarital sex? Having children outside of marriage?

4. What do you think about the role of women in today's society? Do you support women having careers?

C. Political Participation
  1. Are you registered to vote? How many times have you voted? Would you call yourself a Democrat, Republican, Independent, or something else?
  2. Who did you vote for in the last presidential election? Why?
  3. Have you ever worked in anyone's campaign? Can you tell me something about the experience? Would you do that again?
  4. When an election is near, do you talk about it a lot with friends and relatives? Do you try to influence their decisions?
VI. Opinions of African-American Leadership
  A. Political Leadership
  1. What African-American politician do you admire?
  2. Are you familiar with the Congressional Black Caucus? Can you tell me about anything they sponsored or how they influence policy?
  B. Social/Cultural/Political Leadership
  1. What do you think of Louis Farrakhan? What about the Nation of Islam?
  2. What do you think of Jesse Jackson?
  3. Who do you think is the most influential black leader today?
  4. What leader of the past do you admire? Why?

Notes

1. For a discussion of this issue, see Carol Swain, *Black Faces, Black Interests* (Cambridge: Harvard University Press, 1993).

2. See Katherine Tate, *From Protest to Politics* (Cambridge: Harvard University Press, 1994); and Michael Dawson, *Behind the Mule* (Princeton: Princeton University Press, 1994).

3. See Glenn Loury, "Free at Last? A Personal Perspective on Race and Identity in America," in Gerald Early, ed., *Lure and Loathing* (New York: Penguin, 1993).

4. See Everett Stonequist, *Marginal Man* (New York: Russell and Russell, 1961). Stonequist asserts that the failure of members of ethnic groups to assimilate may produce an individual conflicted over his or her place in the world. This individual will engage in contradictory behavior and exhibit conflicting attitudes as he or she waffles from one identity to the other. As the "marginal man" or "marginal woman" works out a reconciliation of these dual identities, he or she helps to reconcile cultural conflict in the larger society.

5. There is a current debate surrounding ebonics, the term used to describe dialects spoken within the black community. In the fall of 1996, the Oakland, California, school district came under fire for adopting a resolution that recognized ebonics as a language. The resolution required teachers to teach standard English as they would a second language to black students whose primary language was ebonics.

6. See Stanley Crouch, "From Here to the Horizon: How It Goes," in *The All-American Skin Game* (New York: Pantheon Books, 1995). Crouch refers to this incident in Tiananmen Square in a very different context. He argues that black protest and political leaders are symbols of the triumph of western ideals about democracy and the rights of men. The story of the struggle of blacks in this country, according to Crouch, is a universal story of human beings striving to live as human beings.

7. See *The Harvard Education Letter* 10, no. 1 (January–February 1994), for a discussion of the resegregation of public schools, racial isolation in extracurricular activities, and teaching about racism in higher education.

8. Davis, a university professor and prominent political activist, was accused of masterminding the escape, which resulted in several deaths.

9. The survey was conducted by mail in November 1992. Candidates for *Who's Who* are chosen by an editorial staff, which monitors publications for information, and solicits suggestions from organizations and individuals. According to the Introduction, "candidates become eligible for inclusion by virtue of positions held through election or appointment to office, notable career achievements, or outstanding community service" (Cloyd and Matney 1990:xi). Of 700 surveys mailed, 257 were returned—a 37 percent response rate. Almost three out of four respondents earned more than $50,000 annually, and 85 percent attended graduate school. Three-fourths were Democrats; 7 percent were Republicans; and 17 percent were Independents.

NOTES TO CHAPTER 2

1. "Hip-Hop" is a term used to define the music, clothes, and language of the post–civil rights generation. While the "hip-hop" culture is shared by young people of all races, it originated with black urban youth and reflects their worldview.

2. Yusef Hawkins was a young black man who was brutally murdered by a gang of whites in the Bensonhurst community in Brooklyn, New York.

NOTES TO CHAPTER 3

1. The "Contract with America" was a document written by the Republican Party congressional leadership in 1994, and included a pledge to reduce the budget and reform welfare. It was signed by 367 Republican candidates to the 104th Congress.

2. African-Americans, as a general rule, do not wash their hair every day because of the fragile construction of curly hair. Over time, the constant washing causes breakage and other damage.

3. An African-American businessman, Reginald Lewis was the CEO of Beatrice Foods, an international corporation. He is now deceased. He authored a book about his success entitled *Why Should White Guys Have All the*

Fun? How Reginald Lewis Created a Billion-Dollar Business Empire (New York: Wiley, 1995)

NOTES TO CHAPTER 4

1. *Plessy v Ferguson* is the 1896 Supreme Court case that established the "separate but equal" doctrine upholding racial segregation.

2. Les Brown is an African-American motivational speaker and author of the book *Live Your Dreams* (New York: Morrow Books, 1992).

3. Benjamin Chavis was chosen to head the NAACP in April 1993. A former member of the Wilmington 10 (a group of young people convicted of a firebombing in the 1970s), his leadership was controversial and short-lived. In September 1994 Chavis was dismissed for diverting more than $300,000 of the organization's funds to a former employee who accused him of sexual harassment.

NOTES TO CHAPTER 5

1. Emmett Till was a fourteen-year-old black boy who was lynched in Greenwood, Mississippi, in 1955. The Tuskegee Experiments refers to the government-sanctioned study of syphilis using black male subjects. Treatment for the disease was withheld from the subjects in the interests of the study. Cointelpro was the code name for the FBI infiltration of the Black Panther Party.

2. Lenora Branch Fulani is a developmental psychologist and political activist who is presently chairperson of the Committee for a Unified Independent Party. She was placed on the presidential ballot in all fifty states and in the District of Columbia in 1988 and 1992. In both elections she ran as the candidate of the New Alliance Party.

3. Gender differences in the way in which minority groups take political or social action were observed and discussed in Carol Hardy-Fanta's *Latino Politics, Latina Politics* (Philadelphia: Temple University Press, 1993).

NOTES TO CHAPTER 6

1. There was one black woman interviewed who was a member of the Young Black Republicans. Her interview is not included here because her

voting patterns as well as her ideology were clearly Democratic. I have no information on how many women may be members of African-American Young Republican organizations on other college campuses.

2. Arsenio Hall is a popular black entertainer and comedian who enjoyed a brief but intense stint as a variety show host on the Fox television network. His show was cancelled in April 1994, not long after the appearance of Louis Farrakhan, due to a ratings drop (*Mediaweek* 4 no. 17:6–8).

3. "Stepin' Fetchit," the stage name for actor Lincoln Theodore Monroe Andrew Perry, has become symbolic of the stereotypical roles Mr. Perry was consigned to playing in at least forty Hollywood films of the late 1920s, the 1930s, and 1940s. An articulate man in actuality, Perry portrayed slow, dim-witted, and cowardly black servants to white stars. Born May 20, 1902 in Key West, Florida, Perry died on November 19, 1985 in Woodland Hills, California.

Works Cited

Allen, Richard L., Michael C. Dawson, and Ronald E. Brown. 1989. "A Schema-Based Approach to Modeling an African-American Belief System." *American Political Science Review* 83, no. 2 (June): 421–41.

Allen, Walter R., Edgar G. Epps, and Nesha Z. Haniff, eds. 1991. *College in Black and White: African-American Students in Predominantly White and in Historically Black Public Universities.* Albany: State University of New York Press.

Almond, Gabriel, and Sidney Verba. [1963] 1989. *The Civic Culture.* Reprint, Newbury Park: Sage Publications.

Ardrey, Saundra. 1994. "The Political Behavior of Black Women: Contextual, Structural, and Psychological Factors." In *Black Politics and Black Political Behavior*, edited by Hanes Walton, Jr. Westport: Praeger.

Asher, Herbert B. 1988. *Presidential Elections and American Politics.* Chicago: Dorsey Press.

Biblical Discernment Ministries. April 1997. "Promise Keepers: Ecumenical Macho-Men for Christ?" http://www.rapidnet.com/~jbeard/bdm/Psychology/pk/pk.htm

Black, Earl, and Merle Black. 1987. *Politics and Society in the South.* Cambridge, Mass.: Harvard University Press.

Bledsoe, Timothy, Susan Welch, Lee Sigelman, and Michael Combs. May 1995. "Residential Context and Racial Solidarity among African-Americans." *American Journal of Political Science* 39, no. 2: 434–58.

Bolce, Louis, Gerald DeMaio, and Douglas Muzzio. Summer 1993. "The 1992 Republican 'Tent': No Blacks Walked In." *Political Science Quarterly* 108, no. 2: 255.

Boston, Thomas. 1988. *Race, Class and Conservatism.* Boston: Unwin Hyman.

Brigham, John C. 1993. "College Students' Racial Attitudes." *Journal of Applied Psychology* 23, no. 3: 1933–67.

Brotz, Howard. 1966. *Negro Social and Political Thought 1850–1920.* New York: Basic Books.

Brown, Elaine. 1992. *A Taste of Power: A Black Woman's Story*. New York: Pantheon Books.

Brown, Les. 1992. *Live Your Dreams*. New York: Morrow.

Calhoun-Brown, Allison. 1996. "African-American Churches and Political Mobilization: The Psychological Impact of Organizational Resources." *Journal of Politics* 58, no. 4: 935–54.

Carmichael, Stokely, and Charles V. Hamilton. 1967. *Black Power*. New York: Random House.

Carnoy, Martin. 1994. *Faded Dreams: The Politics and Economics of Race in America*. Cambridge: Cambridge University Press.

Carter, Stephen. 1991. *Reflections of an Affirmative Action Baby*. New York: Basic Books.

Cleage, Pearl. 1993. *Deals with the Devil: And Other Reasons to Riot*. New York: Ballantine.

Cloyd, Iris, and William C. Matney, Jr., eds. 1990. *Who's Who among Black Americans*. New York: Gale Research.

Cose, Ellis. 1993. *Rage of a Privileged Class*. New York: HarperCollins Publishers.

Cronon, Edmund David, ed. 1973. *Marcus Garvey*. Englewood Cliffs: Prentice-Hall.

Cross, William E. 1991. *Shades of Black*. Philadelphia: Temple University Press.

Crouch, Stanley. 1990. *Notes of a Hanging Judge*. New York: Oxford University Press.

———. 1993. "Our Color but Not Our Kind." *Wall Street Journal* 17 November: A22.

———. 1995. *The All-American Skin Game*. New York: Pantheon Books.

Curry, George E. 1994. "Farrakhan, Jesse, and Jews." *Emerge* July/August: 28–41.

D'Augelli, Anthony R., and Scott L. Hershberger. Winter 1993. "African American Undergraduates on a Predominantly White Campus: Academic Factors, Social Networks, and Campus Climate." *Journal of Negro Education* 62, no. 1: 67–81.

Dawson, Michael. 1994. *Behind the Mule*. Princeton: Princeton University Press.

Dawson, Micheal C., and Ronald E. Brown. 1993. National Black Politics Study (machine-readable data file). Principal investigators: Michael C. Dawson and Ronald E. Brown.

Demo, David H., and Michael Hughes. 1990. "Socialization and Racial Identity among Black Americans." *Social Psychological Quarterly* 53, no. 4: 364–74.

DeMott, Benjamin. 1995. *The Trouble with Friendship: Why Americans Can't Think Straight about Race.* New York: Atlantic Monthly Press.

Drake, St. Clair, and Horace Cayton. [1945] 1962. *Black Metropolis.* New York: Harper and Row.

Du Bois, W. E. Burghardt. 1903. *The Souls of Black Folk: Essays and Sketches.* Chicago: A. McClurg.

Dyson, Michael Eric. 1996. *Race Rules: Navigating the Color Line.* Reading: Addison-Wesley.

Edsall, Thomas Byrne, and Mary D. Edsall. 1991. *Chain Reaction.* New York: W. W. Norton.

Erlich, Howard J. March 1990. *Campus Ethnoviolence and the Policy Options.* Institute Report no. 4: Baltimore: National Institute against Prejudice and Violence.

————. Winter 1995. "Prejudice and Ethnoviolence on Campus." *Higher Education Extension Service Review* 6: 2.

Farley, Reynolds, and Walter R. Allen. 1987. *The Color Line and the Quality of Life in America.* New York: Russell Sage Foundation.

Feagin, Joe R., and Melvin P. Sikes. 1994. *Living with Racism.* Boston: Beacon Press.

Foner, Nancy. 1987. "The Jamaicans: Race and Ethnicity among Migrants in New York City." In *New Immigrants in New York*, edited by Nancy Foner. New York: Columbia University Press.

Frazier, E. Franklin. [1939] 1966. *The Negro Family in the United States.* Chicago: University of Chicago Press.

————. [1957] 1965. *Black Bourgeoisie.* New York: Free Press.

Gates, Jeffrey R., and Robert L Woodson, Sr. 1992. "Jobs and Ownership Are the Answers to Urban Ills." *Los Angeles Times* 7 August: B7.

Giddings, Paula. 1984. *When and Where I Enter: The Impact of Black Women on Race and Sex in America.* New York: William Morrow.

Gilliam, Franklin D., Jr. 1986. "Black America: Divided by Class?" *Public Opinion* February/March: 53–60.

Gilliam, Franklin D., Jr., and Adam F. Simon. 1996. "Crime and the Evening News: How the Media Conditions Racial Reasoning." Paper presented at the annual meeting of the American Political Science Association, San Francisco, Calif., 29 August–1 September.

Gilliam, Franklin D., Jr., and Kenny J. Whitby. March 1989. "Race, Class, and Attitudes toward Social Welfare Spending: An Ethclass Interpretation." *Social Science Quarterly* 70, no. 1: 88–100.

Gordon, Milton. 1964. *Assimilation in American Life.* New York: Oxford University Press.

Grant-Thomas, Andrew. 1996. "All-Male Black Schools and the Politics of Neglect." Paper presented at the annual meeting of the American Political Science Association, San Francisco, Calif., 29 August–1 September.

Gurin, Patricia, and Edgar Epps. 1975. *Black Consciousness, Identity, and Achievement.* New York: Wiley.

Gurin, Patricia, Arthur Miller, and Gerald Gurin. 1980. "Stratum Identification and Consciousness." *Social Psychology Quarterly* 43, no. 1: 30–47.

Hacker, Andrew. 1992. *Two Nations: Black and White, Separate, Hostile, Unequal.* New York: Charles Scribner's Sons.

Hardy-Fanta, Carol. 1993. *Latino Politics, Latina Politics.* Philadelphia: Temple University Press.

Harris, Fredrick C. 1994. "Something Within: Religion as a Mobilizer of African American Political Activism." *Journal of Politics* 56, no. 1: 42–68.

Henry, William A., III. 1994. "Pride and Prejudice." *Time* 28 February: 21–27.

Hochschild, Jennifer. 1996. *Facing Up to the American Dream: Race, Class, and the Soul of a Nation.* Princeton: Princeton University Press.

Hughes, Michael, and Bradley R. Hertel. 1990. "The Significance of Color Remains: A Study of Life-Chances, Mate Selection, and Ethnic Consciousness among Black Americans." *Social Forces* 68, no. 4 June: 1105–20.

Jackson, James S. National Black Election Panel Study, 1984 and 1988. 1993. Conducted by the University of Michigan, Research Center for Group Dynamics. ICPSR ed. Ann Arbor, MI: Inter-university Consortium for Political and Social Research, producer and distributor.

Jaynes, Gerald David, and Robin M. Williams, Jr., eds. 1989. *A Common Destiny: Blacks and American Society.* Washington, D.C.: National Academy Press.

Keyes, Alan. Spring 1989. "My Race for the Senate." *Policy Review* 48: 2–8.

———. 1993. Address. Emory University, Atlanta, Ga., 18 January.

Kinder, Donald R., and Lynn Sanders. 1996. *Divided by Color.* Chicago: University of Chicago Press.

Landry, Bart. 1987. *The New Black Middle Class.* Berkeley: University of California Press.

Lane, Robert E. 1962. *Political Ideology.* New York: Free Press.

Leland, John, and Allison Samuels. 1996. "The New Generation Gap." *Newsweek* 17 March: 53–62.

Lemann, Nicholas. January 1993. "Black Nationalism on Campus." *Atlantic* 271, no. 1: 31–47.

Lewis, Reginald. 1995. *Why Should White Guys Have All the Fun? How Reginald Lewis Created a Billion-Dollar Business Empire.* New York: Wiley.

Loury, Glenn. Summer 1984. "The Need for Moral Leadership in the Black Community." *New Perspectives* 16: 14–19.

———. Spring 1985. "The Moral Quandary of the Black Community." *Public Interest* 79: 10–22.

———. Winter 1987a. "'Matters of Color'—Blacks and the Constitutional Order." *Public Interest* 86: 109–23.

———. January 1987b. "Who Speaks for America's Blacks?" *Commentary* 83: 34–39.

———. 1993. "Free at Last? A Personal Perspective on Race and Identity in America." In *Lure and Loathing*, edited by Gerald Early. New York: Penguin.

Marable, Manning, and Leith Mullings. July–September 1994. "The Divided Mind of Black America: Race, Ideology and Politics in the Post Civil Rights Era." *Race and Class* 36, no. 1: 61–72.

Massey, Douglas S., and Nancy A. Denton. 1993. *American Apartheid: Segregation and the Making of the Underclass.* Cambridge, Mass.: Harvard University Press.

McCall, Nathan. 1995. *Makes Me Wanna Holler.* New York: Random House.

Merelman, Richard M. 1992. "Cultural Imagery and Racial Conflict in the United States: The Case of African-Americans." *British Journal of Political Science* 22: 315–42.

Miller, Arthur H., Patricia Gurin, Gerald Gurin, and Oksana Malanchuk. 1981. "Group Consciousness and Political Participation." *American Journal of Political Science* 25, no. 3: 494–511.

Morris, Aldon D., Shirley J. Hatchett, and Ronald E. Brown. 1988. "The Civil Rights Movement and Black Political Socialization." In *Political Learning and Adulthood*, edited by Roberta S. Sigel. Chicago: University of Chicago Press.

Njeri, Itabari. 1993. "Sushi and Grits: Ethnic Identity and Conflict in a Newly Multicultural America." In *Lure and Loathing*, edited by Gerald Early. New York: Penguin.

Omi, Michael, and Howard Winant. 1994. *Racial Formation in the United States.* New York: Routledge.

Philipson, Ilene. 1991. "What's the Big I.D.? The Politics of the Authentic Self." *Tikkun* 6, no. 6: 51–64.

Reed, Adolph Jr. 1995. "Black Politics Gone Haywire." *Progressive* 59, no. 12: 20–23.

Reese, Laura A., and Ronald E. Brown. 1995. "The Effects of Religious Messages on Racial Identity and System Blame among African-Americans." *Journal of Politics* 57, no. 1: 24–43.

Russell, Kathy, Midge Wilson, and Ronald Hall. 1992. *The Color Complex: The Politics of Skin Color among African-Americans.* New York: Harcourt Brace Jovanovich.

Schuman, Howard, Charlotte Steeh, and Lawrence Bobo. 1985. *Racial Attitudes in America: Trends and Interpretations.* Cambridge, Mass.: Harvard University Press.

Shingles, Richard. 1981. "Black Consciousness and Political Participation: The Missing Link." *American Political Science Review* 75: 76–91.

Simpson, Andrea Y. 1992. Political Attitudes of African-American Elites (machine-readable data file). Principal investigator: Andrea Y. Simpson. 1 data file (257 logical records).

Smith, Barbara. 1992. "Ain't Gonna Let Nobody Turn Me Around." *Black Scholar* 22, nos. 1 and 2: 90–93.

Smith, Robert C., and Richard Seltzer. 1985. "Race and Ideology." *Phylon* 46: 98–105.

———. 1992. *Race, Class, and Culture.* Albany: State University of New York Press.

Sniderman, Paul, and Thomas Piazza. 1993. *The Scar of Race.* Cambridge, Mass.: Harvard University Press.

Sonner, Molly W., and Jeremy D. Mayer. April 1997. "Race Relations and Generation X: How the Most Ethnically Diverse Generation Approaches Questions of Race in America." Paper presented at the Midwest Political Science Association annual meeting, Chicago, Ill.

Sowell, Thomas. 1983. *The Economics and Politics of Race.* New York: William Morrow.

———. 1984. *Civil Rights: Rhetoric or Reality?* New York: William Morrow.

Stafford, Susan Buchanan. 1987. "The Haitians: The Cultural Meaning of Race and Ethnicity." In *New Immigrants in New York*, edited by Nancy Foner. New York: Columbia University Press.

Steele, Shelby. 1990. *The Content of Our Character.* New York: St. Martin's Press.

Stonequist, Everett V. [1937] 1961. *Marginal Man.* New York: Russell and Russell.

Swain, Carol. 1993. *Black Faces, Black Interests.* Cambridge, Mass.: Harvard University Press.

Tashakkori, Abbas. 1993. "Gender, Ethnicity, and Structure of Self-Esteem: An Attitude Theory Approach." *Journal of Social Psychology* 133, no. 4: 479–88.

Tate, Katherine. 1994. *From Protest to Politics*. Cambridge, Mass.: Harvard University Press.

Thompson, Vetta L. S. 1991. "Perceptions of Race which Affect African-American Identification." *Journal of Applied Social Psychology* 21, no. 18: 1502–16.

Toler, Herbert. 1996. "Marching to a Different Drum." *Charisma,* electronic publication of Grace Christian Fellowship, www.pastornet.netau/grace/charisma/c960114/top.html

Tripp, Luke. 1991. "Race Consciousness among African-American Students, 1980s." *Western Journal of Black Studies* 15, no. 3: 159–68.

Tryman, Mfanya D. 1992. "Racism and Violence on College Campuses." *Western Journal of Black Studies* 16, no. 4: 221–30.

U.S. Bureau of the Census. 1989. Current Population Reports, Series P-20, no. 440, *Voting and Registration in the Election of November 1988*. Washington, D.C.: U.S. Government Printing Office.

U.S. Commission on Civil Rights. 1990. *Bigotry and Violence on American College Campuses*. Washington, D.C.: U.S. Commission on Civil Rights.

Verba, Sidney, and Norman H. Nie. 1972. *Participation in America: Political Democracy and Social Equality*. New York: Harper and Row.

Walker, Ken. 1996. "Thunder from Heaven." *Charisma,* electronic publication of Grace Christian Fellowship, www.pastornet.netau/grace/charisma/c960114/top.html

Walton, Anthony. 1996. *Mississippi*. New York: Alfred A. Knopf.

Weitz, Rose, and Leonard Gordon. 1993. "Images of Black Women among Anglo College Students." *Sex Roles* 28, nos. 1–2: 19–34.

Welch, Susan, and Lee Sigelman. March 1989. "A Black Gender Gap?" *Social Science Quarterly* 70, no. 1: 120–33.

West, Cornel. 1993. *Race Matters*. Boston: Beacon Press.

Williams, Walter. 1982. *The State against Blacks*. New York: New Press-McGraw-Hill.

———. 1987. *All It Takes Is Guts*. Washington, D.C.: Regnery Books.

Woodson, Robert L. 1992. "Transform Inner Cities from the Grass Roots Up." *Wall Street Journal* 3 June: A14.

Index

About the Author

Andrea Y. Simpson is a native of Memphis, Tennessee, and a graduate of Rhodes College. She received a Master's degree in public administration from the University of Virginia in 1989, and a Ph.D. in political science from Emory University in 1994. She is currently an assistant professor of political science at the University of Washington in Seattle, Washington.

Many don't have white friends now!